TRANS HISTORIES OF THE MEDIEVAL BOOK

BOOK CULTURES

Further Information and Publications

www.arc-humanities.org/series/book-series/

TRANS HISTORIES OF THE MEDIEVAL BOOK

AN EXPERIMENT IN BIBLIOGRAPHY

by

J. D. SARGAN

ARC HUMANITIES PRESS

This book was published with the generous assistance of a Book Subvention Award from the Medieval Academy of America.

Open access publication was assisted by the University of Georgia First Book Subvention Program.

British Library Cataloguing in Publication Data
A catalogue record for this book is available from the British Library.

ISBN (Hardback): 9781802701630
ISBN (Paperback): 9781802704358
e-ISBN (PDF): 9781802703894
e-ISBN (ePUB): 9781802703887

www.arc-humanities.org

Printed and bound in the UK (by CPIGroup [UK] Ltd), USA (by Bookmasters), and elsewhere using print-on-demand technology.

Publisher (manufacturer) details: Arc Humanities Press, 14 Clifton Moor Business Village, James Nicolson Link, York YO30 4XG, United Kingdom.

EU Authorized Representative details (for GPSR purposes): Amsterdam University Press, Nieuwe Prinsengracht 89, 1018 VR Amsterdam, The Netherlands. www.aup.nl

CONTENTS

LIST OF ILLUSTRATIONS

For Julie, who helps me to be

In memory of Johanna Green, a mentor and a friend

SERIES EDITORS' PREFACE

SINCE THE PUBLICATION of Donald McKenzie's landmark book, *Bibliography and the Sociology of Texts* in 1986, there has been a growing realization by researchers and practitioners of the significance of bookish forms of communication—their wholeness, materiality, contexts of production, and multiple meanings through time and space. This new series, Book Cultures, offers short and focused scholarly contributions to the field of bibliographical, media, and manuscript studies. Our books propose new approaches to technologies of text that contribute significantly to contemporary debates: how can documents, manuscripts, printed books, and contemporary digital platforms and devices be regarded afresh? How can new perspectives on form, genre, multimodalities, and multirealities provide innovative interpretations of early, modern, and contemporary textual objects to reveal different ways of understanding and appreciating the surviving historical record and, where relevant, foreground its distinctively handmade qualities? Book Cultures opens conversations and highlights innovative and creative thinking about all forms of written and illustrated communication from any period and any global tradition. We invite all scholars to participate in this ongoing discussion.

In this landmark contribution to Bibliographical Studies, Sargan emphasizes the many innovative and enlivening significances of trans and queer approaches to the history of the book, and especially medieval manuscripts. Scholars and professionals in academia, libraries, and archives will find much to inspire their own relationships to textual objects, both in terms of the material record and in the ways that this record has been received, categorized, and made to represent normative modes of textual generation and interpretation. Through case studies involving Eleanor Rykener, Jean d'Angoulême, and the Charters of Christ, Sargan provides both panoramic and forensic views of the past with a keen eye on a future that offers the promise of greater community and connection across time, space, and bodies.

Mateusz Fafinski
Bonnie Mak
Elaine Treharne

ACKNOWLEDGEMENTS

IN MY FIRST article on the subject of trans bibliography, I narrated a version of my journey into thinking about this field. In it I mentioned several people who I want to thank again here: Silvia Elsner first asked me how my personal identity related to my academic research, a question that has lingered with me for over a decade. Gabrielle M. W. Bychowski's powerful presentations, especially at the International Congress on Medieval Studies (Kalamazoo) in 2018, made me feel a part of something, without yet knowing what my part might be. I have been lucky to watch premodern trans studies grow and to be shaped by the scholars who contribute to it.

Kate Ozment and Lisa Maruca first gave the ideas in this book wings. They shepherded my initial article on the subject to press, and their valuable feedback opened up the questions I treat here. Sarah Pyke and Malcolm Noble made room for me at the first "Queer Bibliography" conference in 2023 and in doing so they gave me the gift of community, both intellectual and platonic. That community has opened up many venues where the ideas presented here have been workshopped and tested. I thank the organizers and the audiences of the 2024 conference, the Oxford Bibliographical Society, and the Harvard "Symposium on Trans/Queer Approaches to Bibliography and Book History," especially Adam Smyth, Kadin Henningsen, Carlisle Yingst, Colton Valentine, Molly Schwartzburg, Deidre Lynch, and Ana Parejo Vadillo. The 2024 conference at UCLA was hosted by California Rare Book School, who I must also thank for facilitating my course, "Queer Bibliographies." My students were brilliant, incisive, and many of them hugely over-qualified: it was a privilege to learn with them.

The reception for this work has been astonishing. I am grateful to the medievalists who have welcomed the project and been such thoughtful interlocutors. I owe special thanks to the organizers and audiences of the Cambridge Medieval Research Seminar and the London Manuscript Seminar, Rebecca Field, David Rundle, and Julia Crick. Orietta Da Rold offered generous feedback, and I hope that my discussion here does justice to the import of our conversation. Daniel Wakelin and Alexandra Gillespie have been my constant supporters. My work has benefitted from the scholars who received it with enthusiasm and took it to new and interesting places: Sonja Drimmer, Kathleen Kennedy, Bridget Whearty, and especially the student readers who embraced it (and Marion Turner, Anna Wilson, and Dylan Lewis, who I know facilitated their engagement in the classroom). Michael Sargent has been generous with his ideas, work, and images. And of course, I am indebted to

Johanna Green, who was a creative, adventurous, and thoughtful scholar, a kind mentor, and a constant encouragement.

My colleagues and students at the University of Georgia have been patient with my questions and helpful in their responses to them. Cynthia Turner Camp is realistic, enthusiastic, and can always find an answer. Sujata Iyengar, Anne Meyers Devine, Miriam Jacobson, and the audience and guests of the 2023 Symposium on the Book, including Jennifer Low and Suzanne Coley, listened to an early version of the ideas presented here when I had barely arrived. The hard work of my graduate students and the keen interest of my undergraduates have been a helpful reminder of the stakes of the argument. I am proud of them.

The process of securing image permissions is often maligned (and rightly so). It went smoothly in this case, primarily due to the expert assistance of library workers. Ulrike Polnitzky at the Austrian National Archive was quick, clear, and very helpful, as was Krzysztof Adamiec at Lambeth Palace. Howard Doble at The London Archives was generous with his time and resources. Helena Mrkvanová, Věra Slavíková, and Veronika Sklenářová made sure communication between departments of the National Library of Czech Republic was efficient and easy. I am thankful that the British Library has streamlined its processes, and to Katerina Borisova for helping me navigate them. I have benefitted from open access initiatives at the Austrian National Library, the Bibliothèque nationale de France, the Bodleian Library, and the German Federal Archives.

Anna Henderson, at Arc Humanities, approached me with a totally different project in mind. She did not get what she expected from me, but she understood my vision and was committed to getting it to the finish line. Tania Colwell has been a thorough production manager, making the process smooth and my prose better. I am grateful to Elaine Treharne for including me in the Book Cultures series. Dot Porter's reader's report offered the right degree of incisive encouragement to energize me in my revisions. Siân Echard was generous with her words and her time, and without her this book would cost a lot more. All remaining deficits are, of course, my own.

Finally, my family and friends have learned to perfectly balance their displays of interest and disdain for my endeavour. I am grateful that my wife understands my crunch points and is able to show me patience in critical moments. My garden has been a (sometimes welcome) distraction. Hannah Ryley, Alexandra Paddock, Emily Dolmans, and Jessica Henderson, Una Creedon-Carey and Claire Payne have helped manage my sanity. Sidney Herbert (Berbert) has been no help at all.

Introduction

WHY TRANS METHODS IN MANUSCRIPT STUDIES?

> Records, if conceived of and activated for liberatory aims, have the power to change ourselves and the world.
>
> Michelle Caswell, *Urgent Archives*, 116.

THE ARCHIVE HAS liberatory potential, but it is not there yet. The actions needed to get there, archival theorist Michelle Caswell suspects, "will be wild, impractical, impossible."[1] However, they will also be raucous and transformative. Liberatory archives, Caswell instructs, must dispense with the idea that archival work is morally or ethically neutral. Instead, they should embrace the potential that archives, and the objects they contain, have to bring communities together, to reject positivist temporalities, and to use the past to build "a liberatory now."[2] Archives' liberatory power derives from the spaces they occupy and the communities those spaces prioritize, but also from the objects they house and the relationships that those objects have with one another, the formations such relationships take, and the things that we do with them. In this book, I address the medieval objects that we find in the archives and how we deploy them in support of, or resistance to, structures of cultural and political power.

Caswell locates her book, *Urgent Archives*, within a critical movement that aims "to extricate archival theory and practice from the constraints of the oppressive systems in which it is rooted and for which it has been a tool." "[C]ritical approaches to archival theory and practice are unabashedly emancipatory in aim, emphasizing the structural and interlocking nature of various forms of oppression, white supremacy and hetero-patriarchy foremost among them."[3] We recognize the archive—here conceived as both the space in which records are kept, and the curated collection of materials within such spaces—as a political space. In the national and institutional archives of anglophone countries, choices made about what is collected and in what condition it is preserved have shaped and curated a version of

---

1 Caswell, *Urgent Archives*, 116.

2 Caswell, *Urgent Archives*, 13.

3 Caswell, *Urgent Archives*, 12.

history that privileges certain (white, cishetero, masculinist) stories over any other. But renegotiating collecting and hiring priorities in favour of greater institutional diversity, will not—by itself—function to disrupt those narratives. The problem is (also) structural, and structural problems require structural and methodological solutions.[4] How a collection is labelled or catalogued; where it is kept and in what condition; who may access it, where, and when: these are all decisions made by people with structural and institutional power. Critical archival studies uses postmodern critique and activist praxis to surface these choices and the power structures that inform them.

Critical bibliography and critical library studies share many of the same objectives. According to the Bibliographical Society of America:

> bibliography examines the artifactual value of texts—including books, manuscripts, and digital texts—and how they reflect the people and cultures that created, acquired, and exchanged them. Bibliographers study the technologies used to carry texts to readers, valuing the close physical analysis of material artifacts and the social and economic systems that disperse texts in all their various forms around the globe.[5]

The study of books, then, is deeply enmeshed in the study of cultural structures. Critical bibliography, Lisa Maruca and Kate Ozment suggest, "explores how critical theories can (re)shape our histories of the book and bookish objects and in turn how bibliography can be used as a tool to resist oppression."[6] Like critical archive studies and critical library and information science, critical bibliography takes its cue from critical theory, the emancipatory mode that developed out of the Frankfurt School into the parallel discourses of, for example, queer theory, disability studies, critical race studies, and ecocriticism. "[W]hat if," Leah Price asked in 2006, "instead of asking what book history can do for literary criticism, we asked what literary theory can do for book history?"[7] Critical bibliography engages theory to critique or criticize the field of bibliography, its methods, materials, inclusions, and exclusions; to formulate new approaches to bibliographical materials that redress such exclusions; and to deploy both of these things to liberatory ends.[8]

---

4 See Honma, "Trippin' Over"; Dunbar, "Introducing Critical Race Theory"; Ramirez, "Being Assumed Not to Be."

5 Bibliographical Society of America. "What is Bibliography?"

6 Maruca and Ozment, "What is Critical Bibliography?," 232.

7 Price, "Reading Matter," 15.

8 See, for example, the various definitions given by Maruca and Ozment, "What is Critical Bibliography?"; Strakhov, "Opening Pandora's Box"; or Suarez, "Hard Cases."

Formulations of the emancipatory function of critical bibliography owe much to Derrick R. Spires's keynote at the 2021 annual meeting of the Bibliographical Society of America, "On Liberation Bibliography." Spires asks, in relation to research on the work of Black librarians in the second half of the twentieth century, "What use does bibliographical study serve in a moment of national reckoning (once again) with systemic racism and white supremacy?"[9] The term "Liberation bibliography" was coined by librarian Barbara Fister, and draws on the work of liberation theology, an approach to Christian theology developed by Latin American and African American communities that emphasizes social justice as its core mission.[10] "Liberation bibliography," Spires explains, is the "conscious and intentional practice of identifying and repairing the harms of systemic racism, settler colonialism, heteropatriarchy, and other oppressive structures in and through bibliography and bibliographical study." Books and their histories, he suggests, can be a path to freedom. However, methodological change is needed to make that happen: "Some elements of current bibliographical practice may well be incompatible with liberation bibliography, precisely because they are premised on erasure, devaluing knowledge systems, or perpetuating colonial archival practices."[11] Critical archival work, Caswell insists, should offer alternatives, "imagining new ways of thinking about and doing archives that emancipate rather than oppress."[12]

This book contributes to the emancipatory work of critical bibliography through the approach of trans studies. According to Susan Stryker, the cultural historian and co-founder of the journal *Transgender Studies Quarterly*, trans studies is:

> concerned with anything that disrupts, denaturalizes, rearticulates, and makes visible the normative linkages we generally assume to exist between the biological specificity of the sexually differentiated human body, the social roles and statuses that particular form of body is expected to occupy, the subjectively experienced relationship between gendered sense of self and social expectations of gender-role performance, and the *cultural mechanisms* that work to sustain or thwart specific configurations of gendered personhood.[13]

9 Spires, "Liberation Bibliography," 4.

10 Fister, "Trumping Ownership."

11 Spires, "Liberation Bibliography," 7.

12 Caswell, *Urgent Archives*, 13.

13 Stryker, "(De)Subjugated Knowledges," 3, emphasis mine.

The production, transmission, sharing, saving, using, and disposing of knowledge in the form of written media is one such *cultural mechanism*. Trans studies developed in response to a need to unpick the ways that media objects produce, perpetuate, and police normative binary gender formations. Trans studies approaches, then, are bibliographical. Such approaches, I propose, offer emancipatory tactics for navigating and circumventing the oppressive logics baked into bibliographic method.

In my use of verbs like "produce" and "police," I do not intend to position books and other written objects as independent actors within systems of oppression. The idea that objects have "their own agency to shape human action" is well theorized by critics like Timothy Morton and Jane Bennett. Agency, in this context, is relational, and denotes the influence that objects might have over the ways we respond to them. Daniel Wakelin picks up on these ideas when he comments on the effect of material conditions on scribe's attempts to conform to an idealized sense of the text. Here, the condition of the exemplar, the parchment, the quill, and the ink all impact what it is possible for the scribe to produce. Like Wakelin, in this book, I understand manuscripts as not just the outputs of individual scribes but as products that work in concert with local material constraints and wider societal expectations (of the book and the text, but also, of hierarchies of power). When I suggest that a manuscript might "police," for example, socially acceptable embodiment, then, I mean both that books and the texts that they contain reflect the concerns of the society that produced them, but also that they are materially enmeshed in that culture as tools of cultural transmission. Just as Wakelin may look to the form of the book in order to understand how scribes imagined poetic text, we might also look to books as a measure of social or political values.[14] Moreover, what we say and do with books, as demonstrated by critical archival studies, is enmeshed in our own systems of influence. Trans studies, I offer, as a model for unpicking the relational and structural uses of such objects.

For my use of the word tactic, I am indebted to Ingrid Nelson's *Lyric Tactics: Poetry, Genre, and Practice in Later Medieval England* (2017). "In tactical practices," Nelson says, drawing on the work of Michel de Certeau, "subjects find unauthorized, spontaneous, and makeshift pathways among institutional structures." Middle English lyric, Nelson suggests, uses "tactical reliance on and departure from institutional forms of textual production...to shape itself into as a distinct kind of literary object and to reform

14 Wakelin, *Immaterial Texts*, 9–11, quoted at 9.

the structures that shaped it."[15] I am not proposing here a need to abandon or give up on traditional modes of book historical inquiry wholesale—although, like Spires, I offer suggestions about where such methods might need rethinking. Rather, I posit that trans theory can be used to navigate, supplement, and provide alternatives to work around such methods in ways that anticipate, identify, and reject or defy histories of exclusion.

I cast this offering as a bibliographic "experiment." The word "experiment" is intended to conjure some of the possibility of Caswell's call to "cultivate the joys of disruption," and "imagin[e] what does not exist yet."[16] It is also intended as a reflection on the structure and form of the book. My interventions, like those of critical bibliography more widely, are still in their infancy. In this book I stage a thought experiment that asks, what would manuscript studies look like if we attended to trans people and trans method? And, more broadly, what would bibliography look like if it attended to minoritized critique? What would bibliography look like if it shed "systemic racism, settler colonialism, heteropatriarchy, and other oppressive structures?"[17] My answer to these questions is not perfect: it is a starting point. This book is not a handbook or guide to *doing* trans bibliography or codicology. Rather, it is an account of my own foray into that *doing*, which I offer up as an example of what trans approaches to the history of the medieval book *could* be like. It is necessarily impacted by my positionality and hampered by my blind spots. It is an experiment: in joy, in imagination, as well as in critique and frustration.

A book as short as this one cannot hope to provide a comprehensive introduction to either the methods of manuscript studies or the critical development of trans theory. Both fields have extensive intellectual histories; both are varied and interdisciplinary in their interests; both may be engaged as a supporting framework, or as an object of independent inquiry; and neither can be easily summarized. As a result, my treatment of each will—unavoidably—be briefer than some readers would like. However, I aim to treat both areas at a level that welcomes beginners; to make an effort to explain clearly those concepts that underpin my argument; and to signpost key names, works, and methods for those who want to read further.

15 Nelson, *Lyric Tactics*, 4.

16 Caswell, *Urgent Archives*, 22 and 12.

17 Spires, "Liberation Bibliography," 5.

Manuscript Studies

In the introduction to their special issue of *postmedieval* on "Queer Philology," Roberta Magnani and Diane Watt emphasize the cisheterosexist patriarchal models that underpin methods in manuscript studies.[18] In Chapter 1, I elaborate on Magnani and Watt's critique by identifying the oppressive normative models that structured the formalizing of the field—in the form of the related disciplines of philology and paleography—in the late eighteenth century. These disciplines laid the groundwork for current methods in book history, and legacies of that foundation perpetuate in current methodological approaches. However, alternative histories are also possible, and models from feminist, Black, and trans studies provide an opening to imagining a field that is otherwise.

While in life I prefer to think of myself as a book historian, for the purpose of this book I use several terms to designate my field of study, with the intention of being clear about my remit at any given point. Elsewhere, I have called my work in this area "trans codicology."[19] However, the term codicology—which in some quarters of manuscript studies has developed a wider colloquial sense—technically refers only to studies of the physical structure of the manuscript book (codex).[20] The methodological considerations presented here are not limited to ideas about material, form, and structure. The subtitle, *An Experiment in Bibliography*, situates this book within the wider areas of labour and study to which I hope to contribute. Beyond the formalized names of the various Bibliographical Societies, many medievalists associate this term with methods in print-based research. However, as we saw above, bibliography can be more expansive, both methodologically and socially, bringing together a wider community of book-workers including librarians, booksellers, publishers, archivists, collectors, and those with other more tangential interests in the material text. In particular, my use of the term signals both my contribution to the aims of critical bibliography; and my debt to the growing field of queer bibliography, which attends first to the study of "queer material," but also describes "a bibliography which uses queer theories and methods, or otherwise aligns with or activates queer sensibilities," and to which I return in Chapter 1.[21] However, I refer

---

18 Magnani and Watt, "Queer Philology," esp. 252–56.

19 Sargan, "Trans Codicology."

20 See, for example, Stewart, "Codicology."

21 Noble and Pyke, "Queer Bibliography," 152.

most often to manuscript studies. Its short length means that the scope of the book is limited. While I remain hopeful that some of my observations will be relevant to those working on earlier or later materials, I acknowledge that such materials require their own methodological considerations. I am a medievalist trained in the European tradition and the premodern manuscript book remains the focus of my claims. My examples are taken primarily from later medieval Northern Europe, with a focus on post-Conquest England. I also use the term "book history." I do so usually when I am indicating areas of methodological coherence between this book and the work of scholars and critics engaged in the study of other material textual objects.

Manuscript studies, as a field, has a reputation for conservativism. To comment on the resistance successive generations of book historians have shown to the provocations of critical theory has become its own convention, and it may be redundant to repeat such critiques at any length. Perhaps the stage was set in 1998, when Ezra Greenspan and Jonathan Rose, the editors of the field's newly-minted eponymous journal, wrote that "[w]ith the exhaustion of literary theory, younger professors of literature are finding that book history provides a more rigorous and empirical approach."[22] For Leah Price, the study of the material text became known "as a bolt-hole from which to wait...out" theoretical debates.[23] However, critiques like Price's mask a more fraught reality, in which attempts to integrate approaches from critical theory have been frequently made, but rarely absorbed. In medieval histories of the book, such interventions include feminist and postcolonial work in the 1990s, and prominently, the New Materialisms of the 2000s.[24] Happily successive waves of critique have extended the purview of manuscript studies to include subjects like labour, race, gender, and class. However, the incorporation of subjects from critical theory does not amount to reckoning with the theory itself. Kate Ozment notes this disparity across the discipline, where she identifies "a gap between practice and identity, between how current book historical scholarship embraces diverse methodologies and subjects but must do so by remediating a bibliographical history and an inheritance that limits the efficacy of key philosophies and approaches."[25] In other

22 Greenspan and Rose, "Introduction to Book History," x.

23 Price, "Reading Matter," 15.

24 For an example of each, see Robertson, *Early English Devotional Prose*; Ghosh, "The Slave of MS. H.6."; Robertson, "Medieval Things." For more detailed historiography, see Robertson, "Feminism and Medieval Studies"; Holsinger, "Medieval Studies."

25 Ozment, "Feminist Bibliography," 151.

words, scholars have become more attuned to the contributions of women to early printing history (for example), but they have done so by recovering the names of female printers, rather than by adjusting the parameters of the field (by looking for alternative historiographies that include "women's bibliographic labor"),[26] or integrating "tools" for feminist scholars to use in their work. What would a book history that incorporated and prioritized feminist theories of reproductive labour look like, for example?[27]

Manuscript scholars have voiced similar concerns. For instance Sonja Drimmer, echoing Daniel Wakelin, has observed the "lacuna of theoretically driven inquiry in paleographical studies."[28] Drimmer's article, "Queer Transmissions: English Manuscript, Italian Print and a Discomforting History of the Book," calls on us to "discomfort the history of the book," drawing on theorist Sara Ahmed's formulation of comfort as a "fitting in" to normative space. Here she argues that "[s]cholars' commitment to technological sequentiality has long been informed by [the] heteropatriarchal paradigm" of "compulsory heterotemporality," in which manuscript begets print begets digital text. Within this framework, any examples that "fail to satisfy the genealogical model" become "curiosities" requiring explanation. But such explanations tend to reinforce disciplinary norms, rather than resist them:[29] they are cast, in effect, as "the exception(s) that proves the rule." Drimmer turns to queer and trans theory to disrupt both the technological positivism of this dominant narrative, and to question the implicit boundaries it sets up between different technologies (the idea that "a manuscript is one thing, a printed book is another.")[30] She challenges the field to find in supposed outliers—in this instance, a manuscript incorporating free-hand copies of woodcuts depicting the constellation Andromeda with a feminine-coded clothed upper body (including long hair, delicate facial features, and breasts) and nude lower body with penis—"a different logic about the role of new technologies in society" and the ways they re-present themselves as already enmeshed with other book-ish devices.[31] Such challenges address what I,

26 Ozment, "Feminist Bibliography," 167–72, with discussion of this terminology at 167.

27 For more on reproductive labour, including a history of thought on the subject, see (among others) Ferguson, *Women and Work*.

28 Drimmer, "Connoisseurship," 426. See, also, Wakelin, "Paleography."

29 Drimmer, "Queer Transmissions," 7. For "compulsory heterotemporality," see also, per Drimmer: Menon, *Unhistorical Shakespeare*, 1–4.

30 Drimmer, "Queer Transmissions," 5.

31 Drimmer, "Queer Transmissions," 25.

and Drimmer, perceive as a widening disconnect between subject (what we study: gender, disability, race, non-binary depictions of Andromeda) and method (how we study it: or, as Drimmer describes it, "the heteronormative backbone of book historical methods and epistemologies.")[32]

One impediment to theorizing manuscript studies and its orienting structures is the assumption that research into the tangible forms of material objects deals in measurable facts. Such thinking preserves a position of distance that holds our objects and the relationships we have with them at arm's length, preventing us from grappling with the mechanics of embodiment and perception that facilitate empirical knowledge creation.[33] This is not to say that *truth* or *facts* don't exist, of course; simply that they are not innate or unmediated and may not ultimately be verifiable. In her methodological critique of "attributive palaeography," Drimmer presents several models for describing the intuitive work of identifying scribal hands that decentre "verifiability" in favour of examining the "aspect shifts" that prompt attribution. A failure to interrogate the motivations and mechanics behind the methods that we have inherited, she suggests, has resulted in an intellectual catch-22—an "impasse," in her terms—in which the same, supposedly-measurable, features of script can be employed to make opposing arguments. She calls on the field to re-think those sensations of recognition—in this case, of a particular scribe's handwriting—and articulate the shift as a point of departure, rather than attempting to "scientizing" it.[34] Her call pre-empts my own challenge to "take [...] affective embodied response seriously" as a source of book historical knowledge.[35] Trans Studies, I suggest, can help to articulate this reorientation.

Other hurdles are posed by the legacies of the cisheterosexist, white supremacist, and patriarchal logics that organize the discipline. In this book, these terms primarily function as structural critique—a way of describing

---

32 Drimmer, "Queer Transmissions," 7. Similarly, Kathleen Kennedy relates the absence of work on fifteenth- and sixteenth-century English illumination to an absence of artistic theory designed to cope with the genre: such aniconic works, Kennedy shows, do not fit into the representation-based models for pre-abstractionist art. A turn to media theory, she proposes, provides the tools to analyze late medieval illumination in its own right (and not as a substandard version of continental and/or underdeveloped predecessor to Tudor techniques.) Kennedy, *Illuminating Media*: I am grateful to Kennedy for sharing the pre-press version of her introduction with me.

33 For an expansion on this problematic, see Sargan, "Trans Codicology," 574–77.

34 See Drimmer, "Connoisseurship," 456–59.

35 Sargan, "Trans Codicology," 572.

the oppressive systems that organize and distribute power in society and its institutions—not as an expression of personal politics. Readers unfamiliar with this usage may feel defensive about their employment, particularly in reference to a small and close-knit field. However, it is important that we name the dynamics of power within which our field is enmeshed. First, as Magnani and Watt have shown, these structures are baked into the methods and models that form the bread and butter of manuscript studies. Second, as Ozment, Drimmer, and others suggest, they remain central to the unconscious biases that shape whose opinion matters. Trans studies, I show, provides approaches to identify and clarify the field's kyriarchal investments, while offering tools to circumvent their legacy in current methodologies.

Trans Studies

In this book, trans is an expansive category. I follow Stryker in using trans to describe any person "who move[s] away from the gender they were assigned at birth, people who cross over (*trans-*) the boundaries constructed by their culture to define and contain that gender."[36] One critique of trans studies—the quiet fear of many trans scholars—is that our readings of gender may be overdetermined: reading today's trans experiences onto the lives of innocent cis people who did not conceive of the sex-gender-sexuality spectrum in the way that we do today. It is important that trans histories do not reproduce in the past the narratives of transness found in the present. Stryker's approach highlights that gender is a culturally and historically situated experience. Stryker formulates transness as an open analytic through which to understand the ways that normative categories of gender and sexuality have been imposed in various times and places; identify those that subvert such categories; and learn from their methods of resistance and survival.

Florence Ashley's conception of trans as one of a range of "gender modalities" is helpful here. As Ashley, Shari Brightly-Brown, and G. Nic Rider recognize, "[h]uman experiences are inevitably richer than the categories we carve out for them."[37] The concept responds to the legal and medical need to distinguish between a person's "gender identity" ("their sense of gender at any given time") and "how [their] gender identity relates to the gender they were assigned at birth."[38] Of particular relevance in this book is Stryker's

36 Stryker, *Transgender History*, 1.

37 Ashley, Brightly-Brown, and Riger, "Trans/Cis Binary," 294.

38 Ashley, Brightly-Brown, and Riger, "Trans/Cis Binary," 294.

foregrounding of trans as process: a process of "crossing over," inherent in the etymology of the word, that allows us to understand trans as methodology to cut across the binary formulations of gender and sexuality produced by cultural institutions. The term "modality" shifts the focus from gender as identity (which trans and cis women, for example, may share) toward gender as process. Modalities signal ways of being in the world: "a mode or way of being one's gender."[39] In recognizing the processual nature of both trans and gender, this book understands trans theory as a *method* of investigation as well as a *subject* for investigation.

At the time of writing, United States legislators have introduced 905 anti-trans bills—ranging from limitations on gender-affirming healthcare, to gender assessments for children's amateur sports leagues—for discussion in state legislatures across the country this calendar year, more than any other year to date. Forty-seven bills have been introduced at the federal level, in the wake of twelve executive orders issued by the Trump White House in his first three months in office. There are currently twenty-seven states with some level of legal restriction on accessing gender affirming care, particularly for under-18s.[40] In response, seventeen states and the District of Columbia have introduced "shield" laws protecting transgender healthcare.[41] This legislative call-and-response is indicative of the extent to which trans people's right to exist has become a dehumanizing political football in anglophone countries. In the United Kingdom, transgender rights and access to care are also under threat. While reforms to the Gender Recognition Act were considered uncontroversial when Theresa May promised them in 2017, the new Labour government has pledged to continue blocking plans passed by the Scottish parliament in 2022. Meanwhile, the Cass Report, the result of a supposedly independent review of gender care in the UK judged by an international team of scholars to have "methodological flaws" and to "misrepresent[...] ...evidence," has provided cover for the total shutdown of NHS care for transgender youth.[42] On April 16, 2025, in the case *For Women Scotland vs. The Scottish Ministers*, the UK Supreme Court ruled that "the concept of sex is binary," and that the definition of "sex" as it is deployed in

39 Ashley, Brightly-Brown, and Rider, "Trans/Cis Binary," 294. See also Ashley, "Gender Modality," 22.

40 "2025 anti-trans bills tracker." Up year on year since recording began (with bills that made it into law provided in brackets): 2021, 143 (18); 2022, 174 (26); 2023, 615 (87); 2024, 701 (51); 2025 (year to date), 905 (100).

41 Center on Reproductive Health, Law, and Policy, "Shield Laws."

42 Noone et al., "Critically Appraising," 2.

the Equalities Act 2010 refers to "biological sex" (by which they mean, sex assigned at birth). The ruling maintains that transgender people are protected under other provisions of the act.[43] However, following the ruling, the UK's Equality and Human Rights Commission issued an "interim update" to provide guidance on the implications of the judgment. It clarified that the definition put forward by the Supreme Court should be used regardless of whether a trans person has a gender recognition certificate (the mechanism in UK law that allows a new birth certificate to be issued), and that "trans women...should not be permitted to use the women's facilities and trans men...should not be permitted to use the men's facilities."[44] This guidance has led UN experts to warn that "without corrective changes to law and policy" the UK risks violating the European Convention on Human Rights.[45]

One response to current trans political insecurity might be to focus our resources on the present. This is not unreasonable: it is perhaps true that the modern dehumanization and imminent threat to the lives of trans people are not going to be resolved—at least in the immediate term—through a recourse to medieval history. However, when trans people are being forced out of physical homes, the need for a psychic home is rendered even more pressing. Histories provide grounding, legitimization, and evidence that a future is possible, especially when current circumstances suggest otherwise. "There is," observes heritage worker and historian Kit Heyam, "a powerful, electrifying force to the resonance we feel when we realize that someone else has felt our feelings before us."[46] Such affective resonances produce community. Trans histories, then, provide opportunities to build transhistorical communities of care that work to sustain modern trans scholars. Named fields of study develop spaces to share experiences and investments. They offer sites for coalition building among historically underrepresented groups, who have often been subjected to active exclusion.

Premodern trans studies showcases the richness of past trans experiences. Medieval people engaged in sophisticated multifaceted discourses of gender transformation and becoming: from François·e Charmaille's reading

---

43 UKSC, "For Women Scotland Ltd v. The Scottish Ministers," 50, sec. 171. The invocation of "biological" is a right-wing dog whistle and alludes to a formulation of sex that has been roundly discredited: see, for instance, Clancy et al. "Biology Is Not Binary." The UKSC's suggestion that the "biological characteristics that make an individual a man or a woman" are "plain and unambiguous" (50) is nonsense.

44 EHRC, "Interim Update."

45 Office of the High Commissioner, "UN Experts Warn of Legal Uncertainty."

46 Heyam, *Before We Were Trans*, 9.

of "trans climatology" in the gendering of the seasons and their effects on the gendered body, to Jonah Coman's treatment of medieval trinitarian theology as trans ontology, saints lives, romances, trial records, natural sciences, philosophy, theology have been shown to preserve spaces for trans modes of being.[47] Tess Wingard charts the development of the field, which she contends "represents the most important development in the current and future direction of the field of medieval sexuality studies."[48] A growing number of books, edited collections, and conference sessions on queer and trans subjects over the last five years speaks to its vivacity.[49] In 2025 alone, four major conferences have focussed on premodern trans research: "Pre and Early Modern Trans Studies 3 (PrEmoTrans)" at Boston University; the "Premodern Trans Studies Symposium" at the Wolf Humanities Center, University of Pennsylvania; "Trans Sainthood in Translation, ca. 400–1500" at the German Historical Institute London; and "Always Here: Non-Binary Gender, Trans Identities, and Queerness in the Global Middle Ages (c. 250–1650)" at Binghamton University, SUNY. My own work owes a huge debt to the scholars—many early in their careers—who have pioneered and together built this exciting sub-field.

Nevertheless, the material records that preserve transness remain undertheorized. Premodern trans studies, for the most part, has focused on the recognition and analysis of transness in the written and visual record, often via the articulation of trans literary theory. Literature, in particular, has provided a rich source for medieval understandings of gender variance and bodily transformation. But, records of trans people—literary or otherwise—are the exception and not the norm.[50] The trans archive, understood as collections of documents and the spaces that house them, is broadly characterized by absence: both the gaps and silences of lives not recorded, and, as John D. Wrathall has observed of "the archival issues that confront historians of sexuality," the "silences created by the censorship of archival and

47 Charmaille, "Trans Climates"; Coman, "Queering Christ."

48 Wingard, "Trans Middle Ages," 933.

49 Four recent collections in particular emphasize the vibrancy of premodern trans studies: Kim and Bychowski, eds., "Visions of Medieval Trans Feminism"; Chess, Gordon, and Fisher, eds. "Early Modern Trans Studies"; Spencer-Hall and Gutt, eds., *Trans and Genderqueer Subjects*; and LaFleur, Raskolnikov, and Kłosowska, eds., *Trans Historical*. Recent monographs include DeVun, *Shape of Sex*; Maillets, *Les genre fluids*; and Betancourt, *Byzantine Intersectionality*. A rich bibliography is given by Mara-McKay et al., "Bibliography of Medieval Trans Studies."

50 For further discussion, see Sargan, "Trans Codicology," 571–72.

educational institutions, silences created by historians' refusal to acknowledge the sexualities of the individuals they study, and silences created by the authors of the documents historians use to reconstruct the past."[51] A focus on text and image, then, means that the scope of our understanding of the premodern trans experience is governed by the limitations of the textual record and the institutions that document it.

Dealing with absences in the written record is the concern of Saidiya Hartman in her attempts to narrate "counter-histories of slavery," who mourns that the stories that exist in the archive are not about the richness of Black subject-hood, but "rather about the violence, excess, mendacity, and reason that seized hold of their lives, transformed them into commodities and corpses, and identified them with names tossed off as insults and crass jokes."[52] How do we engage ethically in history-making when narrating the archive risks "the contamination involved in restating the maledictions, obscenities, columns of losses and gains, and measures of value by which captive lives were inscribed and extinguished? Why subject the dead to new dangers and to a second order of violence?"[53] What do we do when there is no record at all? Black, trans, and Black trans and quare lives have value, whether they are acknowledged and recorded by cisheterosexist and white supremacist regimes of power or not.[54]

The limitations of the archive mean that when a trans (or otherwise minoritized) person *does* appear within documentary or textual culture, the recognition of their presence is often celebrated as a moment of rediscovery or reclamation. Reclamation is a false promise: "the archive," Hartman notes, "begets a wide array of reading, but none that are capable of resuscitating" those that are lost.[55] Furthermore, as Heyam and Gabrielle M. W. Bychowski observe, the capitalist language of "reclamation" casts archival lives as transactional, as "scarce resource(s)" to be gathered and owned by particular interest groups.[56] Such proprietorial claims are troublesome when gender and the language surrounding it is understood to be culturally situated. They are also, Heyam suggests, contradictory to the ethical work that trans historians are trying to achieve in the name of community: "we co

51 Wrathall, "Provenance as Text," 165 and 166.

52 Hartman, "Venus in Two Acts," 4 and 2.

53 Hartman, "Venus in Two Acts," 5.

54 For my use of the term "quare," see Johnson, "'Quare' Studies."

55 Hartman, "Venus in Two Acts," 13.

56 Heyam, *Before We Were Trans*, 27.

not own or claim members of our communities...[i]nstead we make space for them."[57] What the documents allow us to say about these individuals also raises ethical questions. If the records we work from are hostile, Hartman worries our "own...narration" is tantamount to "further violence."[58] In this book, I extend my suggestion that to read around the occlusions and hostilities of the textual record we need to develop "ways to read *through* the gaps" and understand the capacity of the material object "to act as a vehicle for trans histories."[59]

A more current and pressing need to read "through the gaps" is posed by current political moves to limit the circulation of information about trans lives. Over the last four US school years (2021–2025), PEN America has tracked efforts to have books removed from circulation in public libraries and schools. According to their figures, the 2023–2024 school year saw 10,046 "book bans" targeting "over 4,000 unique titles."[60] The most challenged book that year was Jodi Picoult's *Nineteen Minutes* (2007), a novel about a school shooting that touches on the topics of homophobia, relational abuse, and teen pregnancy. Most books challenged fell into one (or more) of three overlapping categories: books with LGBTQIA+ people or characters and/or people or characters of colour; those written for queer, trans, and/or audiences of colour, usually young adults; and those addressing difficult "real world" topics, such as "grief and death, experiences with substance abuse, suicide, depression and mental health concerns, and sexual violence." Importantly, for our purposes, these kind of actions often happen in conjunction with—or as a pre-emptive to—legislation.[61] In Florida, HB 1069, requires that books challenged on the basis of "sexual conduct" be removed from circulation pending investigation.[62] In Iowa, SF 496 introduces a requirement that library material be "age appropriate" and limits sexual content,

---

57 Heyam, *Before We Were Trans*, 27.

58 Hartman, "Venus in Two Acts," 2.

59 Sargan, "Trans Codicology," 571.

60 PEN America recognizes three levels of "ban": instances when books have been removed from shelves and are no longer in circulation in a given library, school, or school or library system; books "banned pending investigation," which "includes books that are pending a review to determine what restrictions, if any, to implement on them"; and instances when access to a given title has been restricted to certain categories of reader, usually certain age groups or grades ("banned by restriction"). 4,295 books were subject to outright bans: Meehan et al., "Banned in the USA."

61 Meehan et al., "Banned in the USA."

62 For the text of the bill, see "Bill Text: FL H1069."

interpreted by the state to include any LGBTQIA+ positive material.[63] In both states, the legislation has had a "chilling effect" on public education, with more material challenged and more successful challenges leading to bans. In Iowa, school districts audited libraries and removed books "en masse" that *might* breach guidance on "age appropriateness." Here, the "fear of real censorship" caused librarians and administrators to comply in advance with efforts to suppress certain topics and the people effected by them, rather than waiting to be told which materials met the legislative criteria. But in the end, "soft censorship" like this—whether undertaken in the hope of averting ideological and/or material reprisals or not—is still censorship.[64]

The second Trump administration has brought federally sponsored censorship to the table too. The Trump White House has issued multiple executive orders seeking to exclude transgender people from public life by, for example, preventing them from serving in the US military, refusing access to accurate identity documents, and reducing coverage for gender affirming care.[65] References to transgender people and other minoritized groups have been removed from federally run websites. The purge included the scrubbing of Center for Disease Control public health information and data, including fact sheets about HIV testing, contraception, and creating safe and supportive classroom environments.[66] On some websites, the acronym LGBTQIA+ has been changed to LGB, in an effort to exclude transgender people from services and information, like travel safety concerns.[67] In other cases, the treatment of information was more cursory. National Parks Service staffers appeared to have searched for and removed only the word "transgender," so that a webpage dedicated to Sylvia Rivera was left reading, "Sylvia began fighting for gay and rights."[68] Funding cuts to the National Science Foundation, National Institute of Health, and the National Endowment for the Humanities that target projects related to race, gender, sexuality, equity and inclusion, and public health (apparently conducted in a similarly cursory fashion) threaten future trans literatures alongside destroying current ones. And, at the time of writing, there may be more to come: Project

63 For the text of the bill, see "Bill Text: IA SF496."

64 Meehan et al., "Banned in the USA."

65 For a more complete assessment of conditions (available, as they stood at the time of writing), see Rummler and Sosin, "All the Ways."

66 Johnson, "Health Info Wiped."

67 Yurcaba, "Agencies Scrub LGBTQ Web Pages."

68 Reed, "Protests Erupt."

2025, the manifesto that underlay the Republican presidential campaign, equates transgender literature with pornography and promises to criminalize "people who produce and distribute it...[e]ducators and librarians who purvey it...[a]nd telecommunications and technology firms that facilitate its spread."[69]

Trans tactics for navigating the absences, gaps, and suppressions of the written record are needed now. Both the threat of censorship and the need that follows it create the ethical imperative to publish this book open access. But we should remember that our movement away from (many of) those tactics is a recent one. In the neo-capitalist societies of the early twenty-first century, the internet seemed to supply an open space for trans communication, in which self-publication and circulation could bypass the policing inherent to traditional publication routes and bring information and literature to the audiences that needed them. As the above policies make clear (alongside other disasters familiar to medievalists, like the October 2023 cyberattack on the British Library), the internet can no longer be relied upon to provide such a space. However, handmade ephemera, zines, and underground presses have fulfilled similar roles in the recent pass. *Transvestia*, the "first widely-distributed magazine" for assigned male at birth crossdressers and later for trans women, was founded by Virginia Prince in 1960. To protect the identities of her readership, Prince developed a coded identification system that allowed readers to place personal ads, share photos, and communicate with one another, without giving away their name or location. (*Transvestia* also offered a mail forwarding service.)[70] The codes consisted of three parts: a two digit number indicated "the number of the state in which the subscriber lives in alphabetical order"; the initial of the surname given in the subscription; and "the number of persons whose last name begins with that same initial in the order of their addition" to the subscribers list (e.g., Bobbie Thompson, 32-T-3).[71] Many subscribers veiled their identities further using multiple pseudonyms. Prince routinely used at least four names; she had both masculine- and feminine-coded names for use within the community, and a different pair that she used without it.[72] Effectively, Prince developed a multi-layered system that allowed for the

69 Karsten, "Trans Literature Preservation Project."

70 Davis, "Trans* Women of Casa Susanna," 630.

71 Prince, "'Breaking the Code,'" 74 as quoted by Davis, "Trans* Women of Casa Susanna," 630.

72 Davis, "Trans* Women of Casa Susanna," 626.

safe distribution and consumption of literature and the development of a community built on that platform.

Other tactics rely less on a well-developed social network and more on the readers' own approach to the text. As I return to in Chapter 1, such tactics might include an intuitive approach to the book that allows for affective and sensory resonances to build connections; or a rethinking of the ways that texts can be transmitted and received by trans literate audiences who understand their cues.[73] Some such tactics, as the wording of my title suggests (see my discussion of "bibliography" above), operate transhistorically. My comparison, in Chapter 2, between the 1345 questioning of Eleanor Rykener and the 1955 trial of Debbie Mayne, extends this possibility. Others are specific to particular times, places, and technologies. In a recent keynote for the conference "Trans Sainthood in Translation, ca. 400–1500," Roland Betancourt suggested that Byzantine readers "knew more than their text and were working with a skill set beyond that which is written in the manuscript."[74] By revisioning and relearning those tactics, or "skill sets," we develop new ways to resist a pressing reemergent problem: the restriction of public trans and queer literature and the avenues of communication that it facilitates.

Over the course of this book, I posit that by taking trans approaches to ongoing cruxes in manuscript studies caused by the legacies of cisheterosexism, we can visualize the tactics used by trans people to navigate the normative structures of the written record in the past and employ those tactics to re-form the communities they built in the present. In Chapter 1, I revisit the cisheteropatriarchal imperialist genesis of manuscript studies and its influence over current methodologies, before providing a glimpse of alternative dissident histories in the form of roads not taken in the work of early queer, Black, and female scholars. Limitations caused by the normativizing of the field combine with the normativity of most of our material records. Taking Eleanor Rykener as a case study, in Chapter 2 I show that medieval people developed tactics for navigating, co-opting, and reorienting manuscript normativity. For Rykener, the embodied performative repertoire is one such tactic. Mapping manuscript relations is central to Chapter 3. I present alternatives to the manuscript stemma—in the form of the rhizome and the constellation—that re-envision manuscripts as socially imbricated, temporally unbound, and always in the process of creation and relation. Unrooted

73 See, also, Sargan, "Trans Codicology," 581.

74 Betancourt, "Trans In/visibility."

flexible models like these, I suggest, have always been available to readers navigating manuscript relationality. My final chapter draws the previous two together to show that networks of material relation between manuscripts, constructed through the recognition of trans skin technologies, offer modes of trans community formation across space and between times. Those looking to hack the book will find that the odd numbered chapters are more closely engaged with methodological questions, while the even numbered chapters apply those methodological discussions to manuscript examples.

Chapter 1

WHY HERE? WHY NOW? PAST, PRESENT FUTURE

THE MARCHERS AT the "Unite the Right" rally, which happened in Charlottesville, Virginia on August 11 and 12, 2017, carried shields bearing the red cross of the Knights Templar, the Norse *sonnerad*, and the black eagle standard associated with St. Maurice.[1] The medievalism evident at the Charlottesville rally, is just one of the ways that the modern far right has looked to an imagined medieval past to legitimize white supremacist cishetteropatriarchal political beliefs today. Antiracist scholars and activists like Adam Miyashiro, Mary Rambaran-Olm, and others have demonstrated that the early medieval period has become a focal point for far-right groups to project masculinist fantasies of a violent heroic past.[2] In these fantasies, the early Middle Ages function as both an "all-white" point of origin and an idealized point of return. It is important that scholars resist this appropriation of the field at risk of legitimizing racist, homophobic, and sexist beliefs in the present.

However, we should also recognize—as these scholars do—that the right-wing groups who have constructed their ideologies around medieval symbols are not new. They participate in an extended tradition of white imperialist medievalism. Scholars like David Matthews, Haruko Momma, Stephanie Trigg, and more recently Eduardo Ramos and others have shown that the study of medieval English literature, as it emerged from philological accounts of English language, was enmeshed in colonial anglophone interests and politics.[3] The reflection more recent work has prompted in medi-

1 The irony of modern white supremacists fixing on the heraldry of the Black St. Maurice has been noted by scholars. However, as Annie Abrams observes, the alt-right is not interested in the accuracy of their medieval imagery. "Elastic" imaginings of the medieval allow white supremacists to invoke, despite actual genealogical differences, a shared heritage in a past formulated to legitimize and sustain their world view: Annie Abrams, in conversation with Livingstone, "Racism, Medievalism."

2 See Miyashiro, "Our Deeper Past"; Rambaran-Olm and Wade, "What's in a Name?" For a sample of other work in this area, take three special issues: Rambaran-Olm, Leake, and Goodrich, eds., "Race, Revulsion, and Revolution,"; Andrews and Beechy, eds., "Indigenous Futures"; and Lomotu, ed., "The 'Medieval' Undone."

3 Momma, *Philology to English Studies*, esp. 60–136; Matthews, *Making of Middle*

eval studies, broadly defined, is certainly not complete; but I think it fair to say that in manuscript studies it has hardly begun.[4] While philology has been roundly critiqued, paleography, codicology, and other constituent disciplines have remained silent partners to cultural imperialist work. The field of manuscript studies is deeply implicated in such work. In this chapter, I interrogate the founding assumptions of the field, and its co-development alongside other cognate disciplines, to ask what they might suggest about current concerns and future directions.

The roots of manuscript studies within the imperial institutions of the eighteenth-century had a normativizing influence on the development of the field; an influence, as I suggest in this chapter, that developed from the field's enmeshment in the parallel field of natural history, and its investments in sexology and scientific racism.[5] These developments resulted in methods that prioritized measurement and classification over phenomenological inquiry. Sonja Drimmer sees such influences playing out in the scientizing of paleographical methods, and the resultant "impasse" found in current work of Middle English attributive paleography.[6] I suggest that it is also the root of book history's supposed reluctance to respond to approaches from critical theory, up to and including at a methodological level. Both of these pieces collocate in a resistance to grappling with the abstract. Elsewhere, I have formulated this resistance more broadly as a claim to objectivity that hinges on the material, the "fallacy (that) because we study real objects using pseudoscientific observational methods, we deal in proofs and establishable facts."[7] As I suggested in my introduction, an adherence to the idea of the measurable and replicable scientized study of the concrete object draws limits around the questions we can ask and around the impact and reception of scholarship that steps outside of those parameters.

English; Trigg, *Congenial Souls*, 157–86, esp. 159 and 179; and Ramos, "Philology and Racist Appropriations."

4 There are exceptions. An important one that I return to in this chapter is the growing body of work on white-passing Morgan librarian, Belle da Costa Greene: see, for example, Kim, "Belle da Costa Greene"; Gennari-Santori, "This Feminine Scholar"; Lomuto, "Belle da Costa Greene"; Ardizzone, *Illuminated Life*; Ciallela and Palmer, eds., *Belle da Costa Greene*.

5 My thanks go to François·e Charmaille, for encouraging me to dig further into the influence of sexology.

6 See Drimmer, "Connoisseurship."

7 Sargan, "Trans Codicology," 577.

I chart this history not as a stick with which to beat the field. Eve Kosofsky Sedgwick, drawing on Paul Ricoeur, might accuse the first section of this chapter of beginning from "a certain stance of suspicion"; that is, in looking back (selectively) on the early history of the discipline of manuscript studies I establish a position from which the "bad news is always already known."[8] However, I do so to "suggests the possibility of unpacking, of disentangling from their impacted and overdetermined historical relation to each other, some of the separate elements of the intellectual baggage that many of us carry around."[9] This history is intended as a calling-in, not as a calling-out. For many, the manuscript studies of today is so far removed from its late nineteenth-century counterparts that their relation to one another barely crosses our mind. The legacies of this history are not explicit; they are engrained in methodological and linguistic choices. But, as I will show, for those impacted by them, such legacies are ever-present. By facing them head on, I hope in this chapter to make it "more possible to unpack the local, contingent relations between any given piece of knowledge and its narrative/epistemological entailments."[10] To that end, the chapter concludes with two sections that look forward and look otherwise, presenting a counterhistory that offers to lead us to trans bibliography.

A Brief History

Paleography training entered university education in the mid-eighteenth century in the form of diplomatic, which was taught in law faculties as a tool for determining and asserting property rights.[11] By 1765, Johann Christoph Gatterer (1727–1799), professor of history at the University of Göttingen, had incorporated diplomatic into his theorization of Universal History. Gatterer's *Elementa artis diplomaticae universalis* (1798) introduced to diplomatic a classification system inspired by Linnaeus's formalization of binomial nomenclature in the natural sciences.[12] Gatterer viewed history as a system that could be sorted, standardized according to shared dating conventions, and arranged diagrammatically into a model of world events.

---

8 Sedgwick, "Paranoid Reading," 3 and 10.

9 Sedgwick, "Paranoid Reading," 4.

10 Sedgwick, "Paranoid Reading," 4.

11 For more on the disciplinary separation of paleography and diplomatic, see Duranti, *Diplomatics*, 36–58.

12 Duranti, *Diplomatics*, 38.

Diplomatic was an essential building block in that schema and required regularization if it was to prove effective in dating and locating the documentary record. “He wanted to develop a ‘Linnaeismus graphicus’ analogous to (those used in) botany and develop a procedure for measuring time on the basis of diplomatic. (Er wollte analog zur Botanik einen Linnaeismus graphicus und auf Basis der Diplomatik Verfahren einer Chronometrie entwickeln.)”[13] Just as botanists identified plants by the absence or presence of component botanical anatomies, so Gatterer used components of script to date and place manuscript documents. These components were tabulated according to time and place, mapping the interests of the field—in sorting, measuring, locating, and dating—onto those of parallel disciplines like the natural and physical sciences. Indeed, two of the eight founding members of Göttingen’s “Historical Institute” were natural scientists.[14] History, as envisioned by Gatterer, could also be a “precise science (präzisierte Wissenschaft).”[15]

Eighteenth-century methodological developments extended, rather than diverted, earlier foundational interests. The formal study of historic writing traces its roots to Jean Mabillon’s (1632–1707) *De re diplomatica* (1681), a rejoinder to a dispute over the authenticity of a diploma of Dagobert I raised by the Bollandist Daniel Papebroch (1628–1714). Mabillon’s six-book response constitutes the first attempt to present a comprehensive history of handwritten Latin script; classify and describe its identifying features; and provide instruction on dating and authentication from a range of external (materials, seals, subscriptions, provenance) and internal (form, formulae, style, script) features. Book five is dedicated entirely to paleography.[16] A decade later, Mabillon published the *Traité des études monastiques, dédié aux jeunes religieux bénédictines de la congrégation de Saint-Maur* (1691), in which he advocated for the inclusion of diplomatic within the monastic curriculum.[17] For Mabillon, the categorization of script was a crucial tool in the management and security of those great regulators of bodies, the institution and the state.[18]

13 Gierl, *Geschichte als präzisierte Wissenschaft*, 133.

14 See Miller, *History and its Objects*, 80.

15 Gierl, *Geschichte als präzisierte Wissenschaft*.

16 Aris, “Jean Mabillon,” 23–25; Duranti, *Diplomatics*, 37–38.

17 Aris, “Jean Mabillion,” 27.

18 For expansion on this point of Mabillon’s philosophy, see Hiatt, “Diplomatic Arts,” 357.

By the nineteenth century, paleography was widely referred to as an ancillary or auxiliary science. As early as 1784, Thomas Astle stated in *The Origin and Progress of Writing* that he intended "to illustrate, 'the Diplomatic Science the knowledge of which will enable us to form a proper judgement on the age and authenticity of manuscripts, charters, records, and other monuments.'"[19] On the founding of the Palaeographical Society in November 1870, Sir Edward Augustus Bond defined the group's purpose—particularly in relation to new photographic facsimiles—as, "collecting materials for the study of a branch of antiquarian science not yet established on a satisfactory basis, through one in which it is possible to attain to a very great exactness."[20] Such descriptions positioned paleography as a "science," with methods and rules that allowed for "exactness" in its claims, and which underpinned or enabled other areas of study.

Philology was one such area. As Momma, Matthews, and others have demonstrated, philological method became popular among British scholars of Old and Middle English in the early nineteenth century, when Northern European academics turned the tools of comparative philology towards the construction of national heritage. When British philologists produced new editions of medieval texts, they did so in an effort to strengthen connections between contemporary culture and the premodern past. At the heart of this genealogical urge is a raciolinguistic claim to cultural and colonial supremacy on behalf of white English (and by association wider anglophone) peoples. Within the race-making logics of nationalist philology, early England was imagined as a model of white, patriarchal, heroics, and every movement away from the Old English language, as a marker of that purity, was perceived as a threat against white supremacy.[21] The texts edited, marketed, and circulated by learned societies, then, asserted the cultural superiority of British imperialists to colonist (and colonized) readers at home and abroad.

But the nationalist logic of paleography was not imported from philology. In 1704, George Hickes's (1642–1715) *Linguarum veterum septentrionalium thesaurus* incorporated numerous plates depicting different dated samples of script chronologically arranged, which he used "to identify post-Conquest intrusions into, and fabrications of, Saxon documents, lest the knowledge and reputation of Saxon language, customs, and laws be

19 As cited by Treharne, "Good, the Bad, and the Ugly," 262–63n4.

20 Treharne, "Good, the Bad, and the Ugly," 265.

21 See, for example, Momma, *Philology to English Studies*, esp. 60–136; Kabir, "Analogy in Translation," 183–204.

vitiated."[22] The parsing, dating, and locating of scripts was a fundamental support to the philological pursuits of textual editing and linguistic analysis. Indeed, many of the period's most esteemed palaeographers were prolific editors. Sir Fredric Madden (1801–1873) edited—among other things—the Middle English *Havelok the Dane* (1828) for the Roxburghe Club, Layamon's *Brut* (1847) for the Society of Antiquaries, the Old English *Gesta Romanorum* (1838), and with Josiah Forshall (1795–1863) a celebrated four-volume multi-text edition of the Wycliffite Bible (1850). Bond (1815–1898), a founder of the Palaeography Society, edited a facsimile volume of English charters, several chronicles, and documents from Chaucer's time in service to the Countess of Ulster.[23] Sir Edward Maunde Thompson (1840–1929), the Society's co-founder whose *Handbook of Greek and Latin Palaeography* was first published in The International Scientific Series in 1893, was the editor of numerous Anglo-Latin chronicles. All three men served as Keeper of Manuscripts at the British Museum, with Bond and Thompson promoted to Principal Librarian. In 1888, Thompson became the first director of the British Museum. In that role he funded collecting expeditions to Mesopotamia, Egypt, Cyprus, Ephesus, and Carchemish, and contributed to Sir Aurel Stein's second trip to central Asia.[24] He was in charge when the Benin bronzes, now characterized by lawyer Carsten Stahn as "the public face of colonial injustice," were looted by British forces in a "punitive expedition" to Benin City, present day Nigeria, in 1897.[25]

Paleography's cultural imperialist investments and its ongoing claims to scientific method intersect in critical ways. In the mid nineteenth century, the natural scientific typologizing that palaeographical classification was based on turned its eye to the classification of humans. Just as scientific racism employed ostensibly measurable characteristics—such as Petrus Camper's "facial angle"—to both assert the "*truth*" of racial difference and to justify imperialist policies of colonization, race-based violence, and the transatlantic slave trade,[26] philologists and paleographers used the veil of

22 Hiatt, "Diplomatic Arts," 354.

23 Garnett, "Sir Edward A. Bond," 114.

24 Borrie, "Thompson."

25 Stahn, *Confronting Colonial*, 173. For more on the Benin bronzes (and other art objects) and their status in ongoing conversations about repatriation see, for example, Agorsah, "Restitution of Cultural Material"; Gundu, "Looted Nigerian Heritage"; and Hicks, *The Brutish Museums.*

26 On Camper see, for example, Bindman, "*Race is Everything*," 43–49. For more on the fallacy of scientific racism see, for example, Gould, *Mismeasure of Man*.

measurable scientific data on historical language and script to assert the cultural and linguistic superiority of modern English and support colonial language and cultural policy. Their conclusions contributed to the consideration that English literature had more artistic value than any indigenous languages of the Indian subcontinent; that the English language was better suited for cultural and intellectual production; and that Indian languages did not have developed literatures of their own. By positioning contemporary Indian languages as analogous to premodern Englishes, civil servants in India, Ananya Jahanara Kabir demonstrates, made a case for education to be conducted solely in English. Study of the English classics, like the study of classical Latin and Greek in the English Renaissance, would be the path to India's own Enlightenment.[27]

The same period marked the advent of medical sexology. Through the collection and publication of case histories, medical sexologists sought to classify deviant genders and sexualities (at this point considered holistically through the subject-oriented lens of "sexual inversion"). Richard Freiherr von Krafft-Ebing published his *Psychopathia Sexualis: eine Klinisch-Forensische Studie*, the study credited with reclassifying sexuality as an observable scientific phenomenon, in 1886.[28] While Thompson was taking possession of the Benin bronzes, the English edition of Havelock Ellis's *Sexual Inversion* (1897) presented thirty-four new case studies of British inverts. As Siobhan Sullivan discusses, parallel developments in the scientization of race and sexuality "were not only historically coincident but in fact structurally interdependent and perhaps mutually productive."[29] Medical sexology, whether sympathetic or condemnatory in its attitude to homosexuality and gender transitivity, exhibited the same drive to pathologize—and thereby regulate—non-white, non-cisheterosexual bodies through measurement and categorization. "The question of sex," Ellis wrote, "with the *racial questions* that rest on it—stands before the coming generations as the chief problem *for solution*."[30] Accordingly, expressions of gender and sexuality in colonized cultures that did not accord with the binary, cisheteronormative, and patriarchal structures of colonial power, were subject to simultaneous study and suppression. The first chapter of *Sexual Inversion* is dedicated to

27 Kabir, "Analogy in Translation," 183–204. See, also, Rajendran, "Undoing 'the Vernacular.'"

28 Krafft-Ebing, *Psychopathia Sexualis*.

29 Somerville, "Scientific Racism," 38. See, also, Markowitz, *Gender Binary*.

30 As cited by Somerville, "Scientific Racism," 38, emphasis mine.

cataloguing incidences of "inversion" found in nature, which Ellis extends to a range of non-white human cultures prompting his conclusion that "deviant sexualities" were prevalent among "lower races."[31] Incidences of sexual diversity like these provided a framework for gender and sexual normativity to be constructed against.[32] By the same token, non-white people were often excluded from constructions of normative gender expression. When, Sojourner Truth asked, "Ain't I a woman?" at the 1851 Women's Convention in Akron, Ohio, she was responding to the exclusion of Black women from contemporary concepts of American womanhood by the wealthy white women extended that category.[33] Non-white races were not considered sufficiently developed to be classified according to binary sex. Meanwhile, white "inverts," James Kiernan argued in 1892, were the subject of "atavistic reversion," which returned them to a shared undeveloped sexual state.[34]

The intersections of race, gender, and sex in sexological thought return us to colonial medievalisms and their modern counterparts. For Ellis, "true inversion" in Europe could be traced to the Renaissance, furthering a cisheterosexist idealized image of the medieval as "a time when men were men."[35] For England, Ellis—like his colleagues in philology and paleography—takes the Norman Conquest as a starting point for moral (and demographic) decay: in "[t]he Norman times it (inversion) seems to have flourished as it always has wherever the Norman's have gone."[36] Edward Freeman (1882), a scholar of the Norman Conquest, agreed, explicitly coupling "inversion" to the racial imaginary:

> Vices before unknown, the vices of the East, the special sin, as Englishmen then deemed, of the Norman, were rife among [the Norman court]. And deepest of all in guilt was the Red King [William Rufus] himself. Into the details of the private life of Rufus it is well not to grope too narrowly. In him England might see on her own soil the habits of the ancient Greek and the modern Turk.[37]

---

31 Ellis and Symonds, *Sexual Inversion*, 1–21.

32 See, for example, Schuller, *Biopolitics of Feeling*. See also Markowitz, *Gender Binary*.

33 Truth, "Ain't I A Woman?"

34 Kiernan, "Responsibility in Sexual Perversion," 192.

35 Ellis and Symonds. *Sexual Inversion*, 14–15.

36 Ellis and Symonds. *Sexual Inversion*, 18.

37 Wade, "Skeletons in the Closet," 286, quoting Freeman, *Reign of William Rufus*, 159. Ellis agreed with Freeman that William Rufus "was undoubtedly inverted" (*Sexual Inversion*, 18).

For these scholars, just as for the "Unite the Right" marchers, pre-Conquest ("Anglo-Saxon") England was a homogenously white, patriarchal, cisheteronormative space receptive to masculine heroics. As Erik Wade has shown, modern popular imaginings of medieval, and particularly "Anglo-Saxon" sexual morality, compulsory heterosexuality, and masculine dominance have continued to be "cultivated" by academic attitudes. By implying (or stating outright) that locating queer and trans experiences in the medieval past is anachronistic, historicist scholars effectively reinforced white supremacist fantasies about the period.[38]

The events of May 10, 1933, reveal a more visceral connection between trans subjects, eugenicist politics, and bibliographic study. The Institut für Sexualwissenschaft (Institute for Sexual Science) in Berlin, run by the Jewish-German doctor, Magnus Hirschfeld, was the foremost authority on trans and queer health in Europe at the time. Hirschfeld's research included work on homosexuality and cross-dressing, but the institute also offered counselling, sexual health, and contraceptive services; provided office space for activists in both sexual reform and feminism; and had living space for staff, visitors, and patients.[39] The Institute offered gender affirming care, including hormone replacement therapy, for trans individuals, and in 1931 Dora Richter had the first successful and well-publicized vaginoplasty.[40] Two years later, on May 6, 1933, after months of observation and harassment, members of the Nazi student movement broke into and occupied the building on Bebelplatz Square. Then, on May 10, the *Sturmabteilung* (SA) dismantled the library. Photographs of the events have become iconographic of Nazi censorship (see Figure 1).[41] Books are heaped up in disorderly piles, flames spreading through them, until at the centre of the heaps their materiality becomes indiscernible. An inner circle of Nazi officers, including Joseph Goebbels, stand around the bonfires, and outside of them a ring of students, with their arms raised in salute.

The institute's library was emptied, but the books were not destroyed indiscriminately. Heike Bauer finds that "there was a degree of selection in

38 Wade, "Skeletons in the Closet," esp. 293–99, quote at 284. I note that, though such fantasies look backward, they are deeply invested in the repro-futurity of the modern Christo-nationalist state (see Chapter 3.)

39 Bauer, *Hirschfeld Archive*, 81–83.

40 Bhinder and Uphadhyaya, "Brief History," 251. Bauer, *Hirschfeld Archive*, 84–87 articulates the advantages and problems with understanding transness in the Institute.

41 See, also, Bauer, "Burning Sexual Subjects," 25–26.

Figure 1. "Berlin, Opernplatz. Bücherverbrennung durch Studenten," May 10, 1933. Berlin, Das Bundesarchiv, Bild 102-14597. Photograph by Georg Pahl. Reproduced by permission of Das Bundesarchiv.

the process, which suggests that the raid was less about the literal erasure of all of the Institute's holdings than it was concerned with the spectacular effects of invading and devastating a place that had hitherto offered a safe space for explorations of non-normative [genders and] sexualities."[42] Books, as Bauer observes, have a "crucial role…in collective identity formation and its sustenance."[43] Rebecca Knuth has called them "the voice and memory of the targeted group," "central to culture and identity," "vital in sustaining a group's uniqueness."[44] Or to put it more bluntly, as the playwright and poet Heinrich Heine did in *Almansor* (a text that was also burned that day), "Dort, wo man Bücher verbrennt, verbrennt man am Ende auch Menschen (where they burn books, in the end they will also burn people.)"[45] The practices that produce the spectacle are profoundly bibliographic. Witnesses describe SA officers and Nazi students sorting baskets of books and journals to be moved.[46] Some items were saved, and books containing the Institute's library

42 Bauer, "Burning Sexual Subjects," 21.

43 Bauer, "Burning Sexual Subjects," 17.

44 Knuth, *Libricide*, 9: per Bauer, "Burning Sexual Subjects," 17.

45 Heine, "Almansor," lines 243–44.

46 Bauer, "Burning Sexual Subjects," 21.

stamp are now held by libraries in Berlin, London, at the Kinsey Institute in Indiana, and in other places. The Magnus-Hirschfeld-Gesellschaft in Berlin, whose library and archive seek to reconstruct the Institute's collection, regularly announce new finds picked up at second hand bookstores, donated from local library shelves, or given by private collectors.[47] The burning was treated as a pseudo-cataloguing exercise: "with each new packet...a voice declared the name of the author...and pronounced the sentence of execution," 'a French journal reported."[48] (Here, the book explicitly standing in for the undesirable body.) The Nazi men who sorted the books for burning had to think indexically—deciding which titles to leave and which to burn—but they also thought materially: libraries are not actually very easy to burn. While individual leaves of paper can be seen in photographs of the event, many of the over ten thousand diagnostic questionnaires Hirschfield used with his patients were retained. The reason, Bauer suggests, was their "physical form." The documents consisted of multiple loose sheets of paper, some were as much as 336 pages long. "[T]he practical difficulties involved in removing the large archive of unbound, handwritten questionnaires," she suggests, "aided their serendipitous survival."[49] Assessments of size, weight, portability, and ease of combustion, as well as of textual content, governed decisions about what could or should be destroyed.

Moreover, inasmuch as the Nazi attack on the Institute for Sexual Science was an act of bibliographic stochastic terrorism that used queer and trans books as a precursor to queer and trans bodies, bibliography also offered a release from the terror. In Paris, on May 10, 1934, a group of anti-fascist exiles founded the Deutsche Freiheitsbibliothek (German Free Library) or "Library of the Burned Books," an archive that planned to collect copies of all of the books banned (and burned) by the Nazis, along with newspaper cuttings and pamphlets on the events. The library was housed in a two-storey studio on the Boulevard Arago and conceived as "a working archive" and "a centre for the study of fascism."[50] The Library mobilized an international community of authors, publishers, and academics in support including the novelist H. G. Wells, who agreed to act as president for

47 "Sammlungsschwerpunkte." Hirschfeld's private papers were saved by his partner Tao Li, although their whereabouts now is unknown: Bauer, *Hirschfeld Archive*, 4.

48 Gillespie, "Virgina Woolf," 176.

49 Bauer, "Burning Sexual Subjects," 23–24.

50 Fishburn, *Burning Books*, 55; for more see esp. 54–63.

the British "Society of Friends of the Library of the Burned Books."[51] Matthew Fishburn demonstrates an increasing momentum behind the idea of the book as both a resistive and a combative force, particularly in the American press. In 1942, Franklin D. Roosevelt sent a letter to the American Booksellers' Association stating, "We all know that books burn—yet we have greater knowledge that books can not be killed by fire. People die, but books never die. No man and no force can abolish memory...In this war, we know books are weapons."[52] Queer and trans people participated in this response. Virginia Woolf's anti-war essay, *Three Guineas* (1938), takes resistance to book burning in a different direction, casting it—through a satirical, moribund lens—as a rebirth. A series of metaphorical fires (of a cheap and poorly constructed women's college; the house of the professions; the idea of feminism, written large on a protest banner and now no longer needed) make way for a rebuilding of culture and society: her suggestion, that "[w]riters with minds of their own can revitalize a culture dominated by masculine competitive and acquisitive values."[53]

It is perhaps unsurprising, given the views that he expressed, that Havelock Ellis was a member and sometime council member of the Eugenics Society.[54] Readers may be more surprized to know that he also edited early modern drama, heading up the Mermaid Series, which launched in 1887 under the strapline "the best plays of the old dramatists."[55] So, while manuscript studies' involvement in medical sexology is certainly less overt than its colonial interests (notwithstanding the intrinsic enmeshment of the two), the influence of sexology and the power structures that it supported remains visible. Lachmannian stemmatics, the model used by textual critics to reconstruct the order of manuscript copies and their proximity to a (usually hypothetical) authorial original, relies heavily on the mechanics of patrilineal heterosexual social reproduction (I return to this in Chapter 3). Manuscripts are discussed in terms of descent, genealogy, and relationality and grouped into "families" according to their shared features. The pathologizing language of "corruption" or "deviation" characterizes the mistakes, alterations,

51 Fishburn, *Burning Books*, 56.

52 As quoted by Fishburn, "Responses to the Nazi Book Fires," 236.

53 Gillespie, "Virginia Woolf," 180.

54 For Ellis's views on sterilization, see Ellis, "Sterilization of the Unfit," 203–6. Ellis resigned from Eugenics Society in 1931 in protest of their views on sterilization: Wyndham, *Norman Haire*, 192.

55 Krygier, "Mermaid Series."

and additions that mark successive rounds of copying. Diagrammatic representations of such relationships take the form of genealogical diagrams modelled on family trees. The modern field, as Roberta Magnani and Diane Watt observe, "continue(s) to be dominated by masculinist discourses."[56]

Manuscript studies may no longer seek inclusion among the physical sciences, but the "scientizing" of paleography—its enmeshment in the imperialist taxonomizing of philology, sexology, and race science—have methodological import too. Sonja Drimmer, Elaine Treharne, and others have explained the "impasse" produced when scholars come to the different conclusions on the attribution of scribal hands, while citing the same conditions of measurability.[57] But the influence of colonial investments in scientific racism and medical sexology over the foundation of the discipline has, from my perspective, a more insidious legacy. Such commitments impact the demographic makeup of the field by privileging certain scholars with certain backgrounds, experiences, and commitments.[58] In recent years, the broad discipline of medieval studies has been rightfully critiqued for its lack of diversity. The situation is only intensified in manuscript studies. In part, this is a problem of access: until the movement to digitize manuscript materials became widespread, most of the canonical objects of manuscript study were concentrated in a very few privileged institutions. As a consequence, those institutions also became the places where the techniques of manuscript study were passed on. There are currently only two dedicated permanent posts in paleography in England, the endowed chairs at the University of Oxford and King's College London. Tellingly, as A. S. G. Edwards points out, the chairs are housed in different faculties, English and History respectively, and the current incumbents have different disciplinary backgrounds: "in England...you become a palaeographer by being something else first."[59] Such limited options for guaranteed specialist training ensured that the field, and not just its methods, was built on a genealogical model, in which opinions, methods, and scholarly trajectories might be traced from supervisor to student through particular schools. The heritability of such scholastic structures is visible

56 Magnani and Watt, "Towards a Queer Philology," 256.

57 Drimmer, "Connoisseurship," 416.

58 Magnani and Watt, "Towards a Queer Philology," 256.

59 Edwards, "What is Palaeography For?," 23. Other paleographers are, of course, employed in UK universities, but these positions are "ad-hominem" hirings rather than ensured posts.

in the still current terminology of the German doctoral relationship, where a supervisor might be referred to as "Doktorvater/mutter." Here the conditions of the discipline's inception replicate themselves.

As Kate Ozment shows, the effacement of minoritized voices from book history at large is a feature, not a bug. In her "Rationale for Feminist Bibliography" (2020), Ozment surveys the contents of twenty-two book history readers, companions, introductions, and handbooks published between 1999 and 2017. Of the 625 authored pieces, she found women authors and editors to be "globally in the minority" and only about 2 percent of index entries related to women or women's work.[60] The same problem, though untraceable through name data alone, applies to the work of other racial, sexual, and gender minorities. Happily, in the volumes or parts of volumes that Ozment counts with a particular focus on medieval book history and/or manuscript studies, most volumes achieved relative parity, with women authoring roughly 43 percent of chapters overall. But, that figure elides substantial variation: 61 percent of chapters in one volume were by women, there were only four (12 percent) in another. It is also notable that the same names frequently come up in multiple volumes. It is often the same few women who are accorded disciplinary expertise.

I do not mean to suggest that limited conditions of access to manuscript materials are not sometimes necessary. Nor do I seek to undermine the value of specialist training in areas like paleography, codicology, or languages. Rather, I suggest that alongside these necessary impediments to manuscript study, inheritances—both linguistic and methodological—from the field's early colonial interests curtail its appeal, relevance, and availability to many demographics. "As long as manuscript studies...continue(s) to be dominated by masculinist discourses," Magnani and Watt observe, "the field will remain elitist and conservative, as it will focus on ring-fencing privilege and its default identity: white, able-bodied, straight, male, and Christian."[61] In short, the field's early investments continue to play out in how the field has developed; in what questions it is possible to ask; and in how it is possible to answer them.

60 Ozment, "Feminist Bibliography," 153.

61 Magnani and Watt, "Towards a Queer Philology," 256.

A Briefer Counterhistory

In response to the persistent exclusion of Black women's ideas from academic feminism, Black scholars have developed alternative accounts of feminist intellectual history. Barbara Smith, in a radical attempt to define an independent field of Black lesbian feminist criticism in 1977, pushed Black women to "work from the assumption that writings by Black women constitute an identifiable literary tradition," rather than seeking to integrate the work of individual women into a hostile canon.[62] Such moves rethink canonicity with two key aims: to draw attention to the Black intellectual labour that was and continues to be elided in modern accounts of the discipline, and also to constitute what Lisa Lowe has termed a "past conditional temporality"—one that offers alternative considerations of "how we got here"—to present "a much more complicated set of stories about the emergence of the now."[63] As Patricia Hill Collins asserts, "(t)he shadow obscuring [the] complex Black women's intellectual tradition is neither accidental nor benign."[64] Rather ignoring Black women's contributions to feminist discourse allowed white feminist scholars to co-opt the useful innovations and unique oppressions of the Black experience, while skating over inconvenient critique and silently eliding dissent. Such elisions present the history of Western feminist theory as a "monolithic genealogy" primarily produced by white women, and in doing so frame critique of that narrative as antifeminist and reactionary.[65] Counterhistories that foreground the work of Black thinkers acknowledge that Black women have always been a part of feminist thought, while demonstrating the potential for the field and its methods to be otherwise: more honest, more radical, more intersectional.

62 Smith, "Toward a Black Feminist Criticism," 22.

63 Lowe, *Intimacies*, 208. For Lowe's work used in this context see Mann, "Theorizing 'What Could have Been,'" 575.

64 Collins, *Black Feminist Thought*, 3; see also Smith, "Toward a Black Feminist Criticism," 25–26.

65 Mann, "Theorizing 'What Could have Been,'" 582–83; duCille, "On Canons," esp. 37–42. DuCille's chapter tracks these counter-canonical moves across the history of Black feminist studies. She notes the evergreen nature of the need for counterhistory, which must be reformed, recapitulated, and reasserted among successive generations of scholars as the needs and interests of the fields change. The rethinking or revising of accounts of the canon, she warns must not become a way of integrating into white supremacist canons, but a way to reenvision the standards and methods of intellectual history. For an example, see Collins, *Black Feminist Thought*, 266–71.

We might learn from Black women's approaches to building space for themselves, their knowledge, and their histories within and without the field of literary criticism. For, despite the intellectual history laid out above, it is not the case that manuscript studies has been, without reservation, a cisheterosexual, white, and masculine institutional preserve. As Edwards notes, a corollary of its limited institutional presence is that for the last hundred years many paleographers and book historians have operated outside of the academy. As paleography and philology grew apart in the first half of the twentieth century, the discipline of paleography became more institutionally precarious. In some cases, that meant research careers were only open to those with independent wealth, but others "eked out a precarious existence. And still do."[66] Without a cohesive disciplinary identity, in private British paleography is sometimes considered by its practitioners (affectionately, no doubt) to have a history of eccentricity (personal, sexual, or otherwise). "The history of palaeography in England," as Edward's puts it euphemistically, "is in part a history of personalities."[67] "As a discipline," Noble and Pyke note, "bibliography emerged in part from a distinctly homosocial community of bibliophiles."[68]

Women, queer people, and people of colour—and people occupying more than one of these categories—have been, albeit in small numbers, part of the field from its inception. Like many fields that relied on the hand-processing of large amounts of repetitive data—in this case, the transcription, comparison, and collation of manuscript variants—women were often involved in the production of early editions. When F. J. Furnivall and Alfred Pollard published their edition of the Macro Plays in 1904, they worked from transcriptions made be Eleanor Marx, daughter of political theorist Karl Marx who had worked on the manuscript at Furnivall's request around twenty years earlier.[69] Later in the editing process, women typed, checked, and proofed manuscripts, and prepared slips for indexes and glossaries. Many of these women went unnamed by volume editors. For others, like "Miss Gunning and Miss Wilkinson, of Cambridge, who prepared the 'slips' recording the references, and, in most cases, the meanings also" for the glossary of Walter Skeat's *Complete Works of Geoffrey Chaucer* (1894), the names we have

---

66 Edwards, "What is Palaeography For?," 23.

67 Edwards, "What is Palaeography For?," 24.

68 Noble and Pyke, "Queer Bibliography," 150, citing Robinson, "Ornamental Gentlemen."

69 Delany, "Medieval Marxists," 10: see Furnivall and Pollard, eds., *The Macro Plays*, ix.

cannot be associated with any other records.[70] In this sense, manuscript studies in general, and the discipline of textual criticism in particular, were built on the labour of anonymous women.

However, some interventions can be more readily traced, and attending to those interventions could open up the field to an alternative set of methodological investments. Elizabeth Elstob (1683–1756) was the daughter of a respected merchant family in Newcastle. Her brother William, who was ten years her senior, received his MA from Queen's College, Oxford in 1697. At this time Queen's was a centre for the study of Old English and Elstob seems to have picked up her interest in the subject from him. Under William's guidance she learned and translated works in French, Latin, Greek, and Old English, and made the acquaintance of various members of the field. In 1702, she and her brother moved their household to London, where they hosted academics, authors, and thinkers like the philosopher Mary Astell (1666–1739). During this period, Elstob produced the first Old English grammar in English, her *Rudiments of Grammar for the English-Saxon Tongue* (1715). She also edited Old English texts, publishing several editions, including a stand-alone book, *An English-Saxon Homily on the Birth-Day of St. Gregory* (1709).[71] Elstob's scholarly career was cut short in 1715, when her brother and her mentor George Hickes both died, leaving her with many debts and little advocacy among the academic community. Production on her edition and translation of Ælfric's *Catholic Homilies*, then already being proposed for subscriptions by the press, stalled and by 1718 Elstob had disappeared from public life leaving her books and papers behind.[72]

Elstob's edition of the *Homily on the Birth-Day of St. Gregory* offers several innovations to standard practices of the day. She abandons Latin in favour of English as the language of translation and scholarly exchange.[73] Elstob's work evinces the urge to trace linguistic continuity from Old to modern English, but her interest is accompanied by a concern for widening access to Old English texts. Her preface elucidates the connection she perceives between these aims. Old English, by Elstob's estimation, belonged

70 Cited by Moreshead, "Gender and Para-Academic Labor," 1; see, also, 18–22.

71 Hughes, "Elstob," 3.

72 In her later years, Elstob is known to have run a small private school for girls, before being offered the position of governess in the household of Lady Margaret Cavendish Bentinck, granddaughter of the author Margaret Cavendish. For a more detailed biography see Hughes, "Elstob," 3–24. For a more detailed account of Elstob's work, see Gretsch, "Elizabeth Elstob," parts 1 and 2.

73 Elstob, *English-Saxon Homily*, viii–ix.

to a female linguistic history and Ælfric's writing in particular makes the case for women's learning and the potential for social transformation. The work of editing, she demonstrates, is a reciprocal "dialogue between the past and present through which both are enlivened."[74] Linguistically, "she distinguishes Old English by its difference from Latin and Greek," the languages of the male academy, and instead asserts "a more particular [feminine] Agreement with some Words which I had heard when very young in the North."[75] "By publishing somewhat in Saxon," she writes, "I wou'd invite the Ladies to be acquainted with the Language of *their* Predecessors, and the Original of *their* Mother Tongue."[76] Through her textual apparatus and notes she makes the case not only for women's participation in the academy, but for the necessity of a feminine approach to understanding Old English texts. In Elstob's hands, as Kathryn Sutherland has shown, textual criticism became an act of "self-possession" that moved the editing of texts into "the sexual-political arena," asserting women's knowledge and language as vital to understandings of the past, while using the past to support that assertion.[77]

Eleanor Prescott Hammond (1866–1933) was considered among the most gifted scholars of Middle English manuscripts in the late nineteenth and early twentieth centuries. Hammond was born in Worcester, Massachusetts, and attended the University in Leipzig before gaining admission to the Society of Oxford Home Students (now St. Anne's College). She graduated with a PhD from the University of Chicago 1898 and went on to teach there for six years. After her resignation, she taught occasionally at Wellesley College and for a time may have been associated with Northwestern University, but she conducted most of work outside of the academy.[78] Hammond was a prolific scholar, with two extensive books to her name alongside many notes and short articles. Her interests were wide ranging, although she is most well-known for her work on Chaucerian verse form and metre, the poetry of Lydgate, and on fifteenth-century copying practices. In 1908, she published *Chaucer: A Bibliographical Manual*, a 579-page volume that provides "careful accounts of Chaucer's life and canon, of all known manuscripts and printed editions, together with discussion of his versification." The book is

74 Sutherland, "Editing for a New Century," 217.

75 Sutherland, "Elstob," 69, citing Elstob, *English-Saxon Homily*, vi–vii.

76 Sutherland, "Editing for a New Century," 223; Elstob, *English-Saxon Homily*, vii.

77 Sutherland, "Elstob," 69–70; Sutherland, "Editing for a New Century," 213–37.

78 Edwards, "Hammond," 91.

still a standard reference work," the importance of which, by Edwards's estimation, "cannot be overemphasized."[79]

Hammond's name is also remembered in relation to her work on scribal attribution. In two articles, published in *Anglia* in 1905 and 1907, she identifies a number of fifteenth-century copyists of Lydgate working across several manuscripts, including a scribe now known as the "Hammond scribe."[80] Returning to the Hammond scribe in 1929, she identifies his hand in six manuscripts of Chaucer and Lydgate.[81] She uses the scribe's access to exemplars and his ability to pick up copying in the middle of a text, to suggest that this copyist was a professional. More significantly, in several of his manuscripts, he seems to be working from multiple exemplars at the same time. Her observations led Hammond to conclude that "manuscripts of the Canterbury Tales are not necessarily entities, are often of double, even of multiple, source; and the variants of scribes are in part, sometimes in large part, negligible for purposes of classification."[82] Hammond moved away from a model of patrilineal descent that measured a copy's separation from an authorial original in terms of error, toward a sociologically-aware consideration of variation rooted in the practices and working conditions of individual scribes.

In 1905, Belle da Costa Greene (1879–1950) was hired as the personal librarian to John Pierpont Morgan, the financier and art collector. Greene was born in Washington to a well-off family. Her father, Richard Greener, was the first Black man to graduate from Harvard College and became the dean of the law school at Howard University. By 1900, Greene's parents had separated and, now in New York, she and her mother adopted the name "da Costa Greene" and began passing as white.[83] Greene attended Northfield Seminary for Young Ladies from 1896 to 1899, where she was naturally gifted at, and interested in, languages. The following summer she participated in five-week summer school in library economy at Amherst College, directed by William I. Fletcher, the college librarian. By 1902 she was working as a library clerk in Princeton University Archives, where she spent four and a

79 Edwards, "Hammond," 93.

80 Hammond, "Two British Museum Manuscripts," 1–28; Hammond, "Ashmole 59," 320–48.

81 See Hammond, "Scribe of Chaucer," 27–33.

82 Hammond, "Scribe of Chaucer," 31.

83 For discussion of Greene's "multi-axis situatedness in relation to her racial, gendered, and sexuality status" and its intersections with her collecting and cataloguing decisions for Morgan, see Kim, "Belle da Costa Greene," 46.

half years under the leadership of Ernest Cushing Richardson organizing, classifying, and cataloguing new accessions.[84] When J. P. Morgan completed construction on a private library building in 1905, Junius S. Morgan, his nephew and Princeton's associate librarian, recommended Greene for the job of organizing the growing collection. In this role, she "swiftly became the principal mediator among the dealers, experts and museum curators involved in the making of the (Morgan's) collection(s)."[85] She was Morgan's librarian for over forty years.

On the library side, Greene intended that the collection should become "pre-eminent, especially for incunabula, manuscripts, bindings, and the classics."[86] She had a special interest in the first hundred years of print, but she was also responsible for acquisitions that extended the library's collections into areas of interest outside of traditional European history. For instance, in 1911 she acquired two albums of drawings, one Persian and one Mughal.[87] Greene's personal collection of Islamic and Asian manuscripts and art also ended up in the library's collections.[88] When Morgan died in 1913 he left very few instructions. The future of the collection fell to his son, Jack Morgan, and more than half of the art was dispersed to defray outstanding personal and business expenses.[89] However, Greene not only kept the library intact, she saw it opened to the public in 1924, and in 1930 corresponded with Max Farrand at the Huntington Library on shared plans to make "their important original material available to serious students wherever located."[90] In 1939, in recognition of her achievements and contribution to the field, she was made a fellow of the Medieval Academy of America. Greene retired from her post as director of the library in 1948.

Outside of cataloguing and reporting on the library's collections, Greene did not publish in her lifetime. With that said, her collection development policies, personal interests within those policies, purchasing power and connoisseurs eye when it came to acquisitions, shaped the interests of the

84 Foner, "Education," 53–61.

85 Gennari-Santori, "This Feminine Scholar," 186.

86 Belle da Costa Greene to J. P. Morgan, April 23, 1909, as cited by Gennari-Santori, "'This Feminine Scholar,'" 196n21.

87 Gennari-Santori, "This Feminine Scholar," 189; Lomuto, "Belle da Costa Greene," 16–18.

88 Kim, "Belle da Costa Greene," 51 and 55–57. On Greene's "[b]lack [o]rientalism," identification with Cleopatra, and construction of self, see 52–55.

89 Gennari-Santori, "This Feminine Scholar," 189–91.

90 As cited by Lomuto, "Belle da Costa Greene," 14.

field at large and of her particular academic and artistic associates. Greene's insistence on the importance of collecting "examples of manuscript traditions from around the world"—including an important collection of Coptic bindings—appears to "anticipate" current interest in the global Middle Ages.[91] She was part of a network of medievalists, many of whom she mentored and trained at the Morgan Library.[92] By opening the library to the public, she extended that network of interest, positioning medieval art and literature as a more outward-facing, progressive, and open discipline.

To some, Caroline Spurgeon (1869–1942) is better remembered for the advances she made for women within the academy—her part in founding the National Union of Women's Suffrage Society (1897), her position as the first woman in England to hold a professorial chair in English (1913), and her role as co-founder of the International Federation for University Women (1919)—than for her work as a medievalist, much less a book historian. Spurgeon was born in India in 1869, studied at Cheltenham Ladies College, King's College London (KCL), and University College London (UCL), and, in 1899, sat the examinations for the Oxford Honours School in English. She became teaching faculty at Bedford College, a women's college of the University of London, while working on her doctoral research. Her doctorate, *Chaucer devant la critique en Angleterre et en France depuis son temps jusqu'à nos jours*, was awarded by the Sorbonne in 1911. Two years later, Spurgeon became Hildred Carlisle Professor of English Literature and Head of English at Bedford College.[93]

There is no record that any of the people treated here were ever married, but more is known about Spurgeon's living arrangements than most. I will avoid speculating over her experience of gender and sexuality in favour of presenting the facts of those arrangements: Spurgeon met Lilian Clapham (187[illegible]–1935) in around 1895, when they were both members of the King's College Ladies Department.[94] They lived together, sometimes in a cottage in the South Downs village of Alciston, and, when in London, at 19 and 21 Clarence Gate Gardens, Marylebone.[95] In the summers, they were visited in Alcis-

91 E[illegible]e, "Librarian as Medievalist," 147.

92 E[illegible]e, "Librarian as Medievalist," 154–55.

93 Haas, "Spurgeon," 99–109.

94 See Fitzgerald, "Academic Networks," 16.

95 From 1918 to 1929 Caroline Spurgeon is found at 19 Clarence Gate Gardens in the Electoral Register (e.g., 1918, Electoral Registers 1902–1970, Westminster, London, England, P.D.E. No. 4, Dorset Square and Regent's Park Ward, Div. 1, p. 10, no. 9[illegible]2, Spurgeon, Caroline Frances Eleanor). Over the same period (until 1930),

ton by Virginia Gildersleeve, Dean of Barnard College, and in the autumn or winter Spurgeon would make the return trip to New York.[96] She listed Clapham as her next of kin when making these visits.[97] When Clapham died in 1935, Spurgeon erected a gravestone in the village "in grateful remembrance of forty years of steadfast friendship and of happy life together." After Clapham's death, Spurgeon moved with Gildersleeve to Tucson, Arizona, where she died in 1942. In accordance with her wishes, after World War II had ended Gildersleeve had Spurgeon's ashes removed back to Alciston to be buried next to Clapham in a shared plot.[98]

Spurgeon's three-volume monograph, *Five Hundred Years of Chaucer Criticism and Allusion 1375–1900* (1925), was a pioneering investigation of the history of reception, which catalogues "all the opinions that could

---

Lilian Mary Clapham is registered at 21 Clarence Gate Gardens (e.g., 1918, Electoral Registers 1902–1970, Westminster, London, England, P.D.E. No. 4, Dorset Square and Regent's Park Ward, Div. 1, p. 10, no. 954, Clapham, Lilian Mary). From 1927 to 1939, Spurgeon was also registered at Old Postman's Cottage, Alciston, East Sussex, with Clapham registered there from 1931 to 1936 (e.g., Electoral Registers, 1705–1963, East Sussex, England, Eastbourne, P.D.M, Parish of Alciston, p. 2, no. 21, Clapham, Lilian Mary, and p. 3, no. 10, Spurgeon, Caroline Frances Eleanor). Together, they are at 19 Clarence Gate Gardens, for both available census in this period: London, The National Archives, Census of England and Wales, 1911, London, Marylebone, 19 Clarence Gate Gardens, schedule 354, Spurgeon, Caroline F. E.; London, The National Archives, Census of England and Wales, 1921, London, Marylebone, 19 Clarence Gate Gardens, schedule 353, Clapham, Lilian Mary. In 1921 Spurgeon was not present on the day of the census, but a gap has been left in the first slot on the return, as if anticipating her position as "head" of the household (where she appears in 1911). The prefilled address on the back of the return has her name, which was neatly crossed out and replaced with Clapham's when it became clear that Spurgeon would not be filling it in. In 1911, 21 Clarence Gate Gardens was home to Mildred May Nickalls; in 1921, no return was filed at that address.

96 Fitzgerald, "Academic Networks," 16–17. Spurgeon and Clapham kept a guest book at Old Postman's Cottage, which is now East Sussex and Brighton and Hove Records Office, AMS6516/7.

97 At some points during the period that Spurgeon was visiting the US, ships asked for the name and address of passengers' "nearest relative or friend" in the country of origin. See, for example US Department of Labor, Arriving Passenger and Crew Lists, 1820–1957, List or Manifest of Alien Passengers for the United States, S.S. Carmania, Passengers Sailing from Southampton, December 17, 1921, List 4, no. 5, Spurgeon, Caroline F. E. In December 1933, Spurgeon and Clapham travelled together.

98 Fitzgerald, "Academic Networks," 17. Spurgeon and Clapham's heads ones are next to each other in the graveyard at Alciston Church, Alciston, East Sussex. Gildersleeve is buried with Elizabeth Reynard under a shared headstone in the cemetery of St. Matthew's Episcopal Church, Bedford, New York.

be gathered on Chaucer."[99] The book is part reference work, part analytical investigation, presenting a diachronic study of trends in critical opinions, citations, and references to Chaucer's works based on a huge volume and variety of documents. In many ways, the study anticipates the modern rubric of distant reading, or so-called "big data" approaches to book history.[100] Her work on Shakespeare's imagery extends this method. In *Shakespeare's Imagery, and What it Tells Us* (1935), she produces a stylometric analysis that quantifies various word clusters across Shakespeare's plays as a measure of different signature interests and ideas over his canon.[101] Her conclusions, then, consider the role of the individual in the creation, transmission, and reception of the text, and by extension, the status of the critic both as an individual reader and as a product of a historically contingent reading culture. Spurgeon's interest in reading and reception extends to her more traditionally book historical work. Her short volume, *Keats's Shakespeare* (1928), comprises a description and commentary on the nine volumes of Shakespeare owned by the poet John Keats, with particular focus on his annotations.[102] Here, the material form of the book becomes a tool for the analysis of literary influence and the development and transmission of imagery.

The four people discussed in this chapter represent just a fraction of the contributions made to the field by individuals who were not cisheterosexual, white, and male. Others are less well documented. Projects like the "Women in Book History Bibliography" edited by Cait Coker and Kate Ozment, or the "Black Bibliography Project" directed by Jacqueline Goldsby and Meredith McGill work to resurface the contributions of those who have historically been undercredited. However, it is likely that the labour—physical and intellectual—of women like "Miss Gunning and Miss Wilkinson" will never be fully recovered. Elstob, Hammond, Greene, and Spurgeon are people about whom we possess a certain amount of knowledge, due often—at least in part—to their patronage by wealthy or socially and institutionally respected men. They benefitted from and contributed to the kyriarchical standards of the field, as well as being taken advantage of by them. Elstob was wealthy until she was not; she enjoyed the freedom of following her interests with

99 Spurgeon, *Five Hundred Years.*

100 For distant reading, see Moretti, "Style, Inc.," 134–58. For approaches to "big data" in manuscript studies see "Big Data and Manuscript Studies," ed. Mattison and Ripley.

101 Spurgeon, *Shakespeare's Imagery.*

102 Spurgeon, *Keats's Shakespeare.*

the support of her brother and other well-off academic patrons. Spurgeon lost her parents as a small child, but as the well-educated, Indian-born daughter of an army Captain, she was, as Nancy Woloch has said of Virginia Gildersleeve, "a consummate insider":[103] the picture of "an (upper-) middle-class daughter of the British Empire."[104] As the daughter of an academic turned diplomat, Greene too was born into relative privilege; though this, as Dorothy Kim has shown, did not put the family above racialized precarity.[105] Her ability to pass as white granted her access to the elite world of New York art collecting, but did not remove the necessity of balancing personal, ethical, and practical commitments with the interests and aspirations of her employer-cum-patron. Consequently, Greene's collection at the Morgan Library was typical of the manuscript interests of the early twentieth-century academy: it is primarily a "white heritage collection for the agenda of white, American industrialists."[106] Nevertheless, each found tactics to navigate and adapt disciplinary norms, and a field built with attention to their work might be more open about its investments, less susceptible to patriarchal assumptions, think more transhistorically and transregionally about the past, and acknowledge the reciprocity of our relationships with it.

Queer Bibliography, Trans Bibliography

Queer and trans people have always engaged in bibliographic practice, Sarah Pyke and Malcolm Noble point out in the introduction to a 2024 special issue on Queer Bibliography. In the period discussed above, we might think—as Noble and Pyke do—of Stephen Gordon in Radclyffe Hall's *The Well of Loneliness* (1928), whose queerness, figured by Hall as "sexual inversion," implicates both gender and sexual non-normativity ("I must be a boy, 'cause I feel exactly like one," Stephen tells the housemaid, Collins).[107] Reading her father's marginalia in a copy of Krafft-Ebing's *Psychopathia Sexualis* (1886) prompts a recognition that both registers the queerness she already feels, and shapes the path of the rest of her life. Reading the signs

103 Woloch, *The Insider*, 51.

104 Haas, "Spurgeon," 99. Spurgeon received an army pension of £12 a year from 1873 to 1891: see Royal Hospital Chelsea, Compassionate Allowances, Royal Bounty and Relief Fund, WO 23/116, no. 42, paper no. 70918/9.

105 Kim, "Belle da Costa Greene," 44–46.

106 Kim, "Belle da Costa Greene," 47.

107 Hall, *Well of Loneliness*, 14.

of her father reading sexology, for Stephen, shows her that she was always already queer.[108] "[Q]ueer bibliographical labor and expertise," Noble and Pyke show, "have always existed, in professionalized and amateur forms, even if queer bibliography is only now emerging in a new disciplinary formation."[109] Queer people understand the power of texts as material forms to shape, share, and transmit identity; and queer readers develop the ability to read with, through, and counter to the form of the book, in order to identify material likely to provide self-recognition. For modern queers, intuitive approaches to the identification of queer content might include "poring over covers, colophons, and card catalogs, decoding, chasing clues, following tenuous 'threads of connection' from material text to material text."[110] For many queer bibliographers, the intuitive material approaches they developed as young people led to formalized studies of book objects that foreground the haptic and affective qualities of that engagement. This book contends that premodern queer and trans people also understood the power of the material text to construct gender and sexuality through active embodied use (see esp. Chapter 4).

The presence or absence of trans lives in the documentary record has primarily been theorized by librarians and archivists. Research in this area can be divided into several key themes. One concern is access: it does not matter whether material is in an archive, if no one is able to find and use that material. For material to be findable, it must be catalogued and tagged using appropriate and comprehensible terminology and/or equipped with clear and non-pathologizing bibliographical classification (the call number that designates where a book is filed on the shelf and the language used to describe its content). As Melissa Adler points out, before the 1970s books with queer characters or storylines would have been catalogued under the subject heading "sexual perversion." At that time, activists inside and outside the "Task Force on Gay Liberation" of the American Library Association, like Barbara Gittings, Joan Marshall, and Steve Wolf, pursued the Library of Congress to change cataloguing standards. Librarians realized, Adler reminds us, that "dominant heteronormative discourses relied upon and were enforced by subject classifications," and that "categories both open and close fields of possibility. In the library, this ongoing dialectic brings subjects

108 Hall, *Well of Loneliness*, 231; Noble and Pyke, "Queer Bibliography," 155; see Rohy, *Lost Causes*, 123.

109 Noble and Pyke, "Queer Bibliography," 153. See, also, Noble and Pyke, "Bibliographical Gathering."

110 Noble and Pyke, "Queer Bibliography," 154.

into being on the library shelves while simultaneously positioning the user in relation to documents and the system of categorization."[111] You cannot be what you cannot see. But decisions about what new terms we ascribe to a record also have consequences, K. J. Rawson points out. Deploying terms like "transgender" too liberally, or too conservatively, risks speaking for people who have not been allowed to speak for themselves and thereby isolating those records from the histories they belong to. The project to negotiate expanding identity categories while reducing harm in the ways information about race, gender, and sexuality are organized and assigned in libraries and archives continues through projects like the *Homosaurus*, "an international linked data vocabulary" of LGBTQ+ terms intended to "function as a companion to broad subject term vocabularies," "enhancing discoverability" by providing breadth while standardizing and advising on terminology.[112] Queer and trans archival studies, then, acknowledges the need for a revisioning of the historical record, and the way such documents participate in structures of power.

Access, Rawson observes, is also about the space, shape, and time of the archive: archival spaces shape how researchers interact with records. The Sexual Minorities Archive, Rawson suggests—where archival objects are permanently on display with minimal interpretative metadata—presents a model of discovery in which objects are allowed to "speak to" the researcher, "embracing a different kind of satisfaction that recognizes that collections can have desires and want to be touched, too."[113] Similarly, the lived-in archive presented by Tom of Finland House puts visitors in intimate relation with the erotic art and ephemera on show, blurring the distinctions between archival objects, household tools, tongue-in-cheek play things, and ephemeral pornography.[114] Many of these encounters could take place *only* outside

---

111 Adler, "Let's not Homosexualize," 503.

112 *Homosaurus.*

113 Rawson, "Desiring Queer(er?) Archival Logics," 137.

114 Tom of Finland House at 1421 Laveta Terrace, Los Angeles was the home of celebrated erotic artist Tom of Finland (Touko Laaksonen, 1920–1991) and is still the residence of his one-time partner Durk Dehner and Dehner's long-term partner Spike, as well as several resident artists at any one time. It is also the world's largest repository of homoerotic art, and houses a functioning library and archive run by Marti Pike. For the purposes of this book, Pike's work at the library, which includes establishing a catalogue and classmark system that could cope with the diverse collection of source material Tom used in his work and make meaningful differentiations between a wide assortment of erotic and pornographic materials should be better known. The collection is spread throughout the house, with the main

of the institutional setting, in community archives that build trust, understanding, and even overlap between patrons and those caring for the collection. However, such reimaginings of the object-encounter are instructive. At Tom of Finland house, living with the collection is generative: it is part of the creative inspiration for artists participating in the Tom of Finland Foundation's in-house residency scheme. Rawson posits that alternative modes of archival access like these constitute "a queer revision of traditional historiographic method…that is based on the ways that researchers *feel* archives and *desire* history, and the ways that archives and history feel and desire right back."[115] The reciprocated touch of the archive—famously figured by Carolyn Dinshaw as "the queer historical impulse…toward making connections across time"—complicates the linear temporality presented by western historiographies, especially in the hands of transgender researchers, whose identification with archival materials may carry the shame, fear, or anguish borne of current oppressions in lieu of the pleasure of recognition.[116]

Finally, such spaces are negotiated by embodied subjects. This book takes its cue, in particular, from Susan Stryker's reminder that "embodiment not only animates the research query but modulates access to the archive, in both its physical and its intellectual arrangement."[117] Rawson and Charles E. Morris III recognize the reciprocal relationship between archive and body in their formulation of the "archival queer." Archival queers "resist the archive as a purely intellectual space and…seek out affective relations with the past."[118] For example, Marika Cifor recalls "the intoxicating affective mixture of surprise and (dis)pleasure" she felt on encountering a hair belonging to trans sex worker and activist, Victoria Schneider, while going through the contents of Schneider's makeup bag in the Gay, Lesbian, Bisexual, and Transgender Historical Society's (GLBTHS) reading room. For Cifor, the hair, as a piece of bodily ephemera, animated the bodily violation that Schneider experienced, but it was her own embodied response that "alters

library room (which houses Pike's database and about two thirds of the Foundation's books, including most of Tom of Finland's original publications) situated next door to the communal bathroom, enmeshing it within the fabric of the daily life of getting up and getting out in a multi-person household.

115 Rawson, "Desiring Queer(er?) Archival Logics," 137.

116 Dinshaw, *Getting Medieval*, 1. See Rawson, "Desiring Queer(er?) Archival Logics," 139 Love, *Feeling Backward*.

117 Stryker, "Homonormativity, and Disciplinarity," 153. See also Kirsch and Rohan, eds., *Beyond the Archives*.

118 Rawson and Morris, "Queer Archives/Archival Queers," 80.

[Cifor's] identification with Victoria in appropriately messy and uncomfortable ways, calling attention to [her] privileges (gender, class, education) and the dangers of identification in erasing meaningful differences."[119] As I have suggested elsewhere, then, embodied experience is a crucial stage in the acquisition of knowledge: "Research is, in the spirit of true Baconian empiricism, simply a series of sensory inputs and outputs."[120] Trans and queer bodies accrue across their lifetimes a shifting range of experiences unavailable to their cishetero counterparts: the embodied experiences we bring to the archive, and the affective resonances they facilitate, are fundamental for recognizing alternate ways of knowing.

Noble and Pyke's introduction converts these archival considerations into a series of preliminary precepts—intellectual and ethical—intended to delineate expectations for queer bibliography as a sub-field:

> *Queer bibliography centres affect and embodiment.* It attends to how and what printed matter makes us feel, and it wonders how material felt in queer historical hands.
>
> *Queer bibliography intuits.* It amplifies the minute material, paratextual, and textual signals steering receptive readers in the right direction, attuned to hints and traces, the coded and the unsaid, the "bat's squeak of sexuality." It listens to silences very carefully.
>
> *Queer bibliography is messy and speculative.* It strives to describe material texts' resonances, qualities, or techniques that may resist easy expression; it can be tentative, or pluralistic and rich. It sometimes overspills the limits of existing training, conventions, and infrastructures.
>
> *Queer bibliography takes place inside and outside universities, libraries, archives, and other institutional settings.* Practitioners need not be academics, nor have formal training. Queer bibliography is being carried out by book artists, printers, booksellers, and by communities of young people on Instagram and on TikTok who have developed their own book cultures and protocols. These may be viewed aslant as a form of para-academic, wholly unorthodox—though rigorous—"peer review."[121]

These tenets remain true for trans book history. Trans studies shares the queer commitment to liberation from normative frameworks of gender and sexuality, and in this book I will often deploy the words "trans and queer"

---

119 Cifor, "Presence, Absence, and Victoria's Hair," 248.

120 Sargan, "Trans Codicology," 576.

121 Noble and Pyke, "Queer Bibliography," 166.

simultaneously. However, I propose some additional parameters of my own also, using Noble and Pyke's model as a starting point but guided by the particular (sometimes divergent) interests and approaches of trans studies. For Stryker, trans studies was born as "queer theory's evil twin": disrupting and refusing to stabilize the gender systems on which sexuality is built.[122] I take special note of trans studies' particular interest in the *processes* and *techniques* of embodiment. "Queer," Heather Love comments, "has proven less useful than transgender studies in accounting for embodiment. Trans studies makes accounting for material experience and making space for new forms and experiences of embodiment central."[123] Finally, as Andrea Long Chu and Emmett Harsin Drager hypothesize in their state-of-the-field discussion "After Trans Studies," transness knows what it is to make and break norms: "what it means to be attached to a norm—by desire, by habit, by survival." Trans studies offers more ambivalent approaches to what is normative, and to how community might be constructed in, through, and around normative modes.[124]

> *Trans bibliography reveals normative models.*
>
> *Trans bibliography fosters connection and community formation.*
>
> *Trans bibliography emphasizes process.*
>
> *Trans bibliography is materially engaged.*

I have used these guidelines as a roadmap to the chapters that follow. Of course, the presence of most of them will be felt in more than one chapter, but each chapter is conceived to foreground one tenet in particular. This chapter began by exposing and rethinking the foundations of the field in white patriarchal imperialism and thinking through some of the normativizing legacies that history has left behind. Chapter 2 is premised on the normativity of the manuscript record and the tactics trans people have employed to navigate such records. Chapter 3 proposes a framework to reformulate relations between manuscripts, situating the material text as a processual and connective force. The fourth chapter brings together these ideas to put forward embodied touch as a tactic that turns normative manuscripts into tools of trans and queer community formation, both in the past and today.

---

122 Stryker, "Transgender Studies."

123 Love, "Queer," 175.

124 Chu and Drager, "After Trans Studies," 108.

Chapter 2

NAVIGATING NORMATIVE BOOKS

IT IS TEMPTING to imagine all medieval manuscripts as trans or queer products. If we understand queer as a broad category indicating deviation from a set of normative values, it is easy to begin noticing such deviations in manuscripts. Manuscript transmission, for instance, is defined, according to Bernard Cerquiglini, by its variation, resulting in "l'excès joyeux (joyful excess[es])."[1] Cerquiglini's celebration of the joy of the variant manuscript text, chimes with the concept of *jouissance* in Continental theory, which registers transgressive and unregulated (excessive) pleasure. Meanwhile, for Lachmannian stemmatics (as I return to in Chapter 3) the variant transgresses the normative bounds of the authorial text. Such excesses (joyous, transgressive, or otherwise), might strike Susan Sontag as camp: "exaggerated," "attenuated," "outrageous," "playful," "slight[ing] content" in favour of style and crucially for Sontag, "unintentional" and "naïve."[2] Eve Kosofsky Sedgwick, in her consideration of reparative reading, understands classic camp performance as including, "the 'over'-attachment to fragmentary, marginal, waste, or leftover products."[3] Certainly, manuscript culture can be and do all of these things: are all manuscripts a campy field of gender play?

Every manuscript is handmade and so necessarily distinct from every other. Curator and theorist Jeanne Vaccaro connects "transgender corporealities to labor and the politics of the handmade" in order to reclaim trans identity production as processual and embodied, and "counter biomedical and psychological discourses that pathologize non-normative transgender transitions, and the body's dependence on external technologies."[4] For Vaccaro, the trans experience is a handmade experience in a constant state of *becoming* through "affective, textured and dimensional labor."[5] In her approach to visible handmadeness and handicraft in queer and trans

1 Cerquiglini, *Éloge de la variante*, 55–69; trans. Wing, *In Praise of the Variant*, 33–45.

2 Sontag, "Notes on 'Camp.'"

3 Sedgwick, "Paranoid Reading," 28.

4 Vaccaro, "Felt Matters," 254.

5 Vaccaro, "Felt Matters," 255.

art, then, Vaccaro looks to "materializ[e] alternative...affective economies and networks of relationality."[6] Such commitments also echo the remit of book history, which Robert Darnton defines as the analysis of the "communications circuit that runs from the author to the publisher...the printer, the shipper, the bookseller, and the reader...Book history concerns each phase of this process and the process as a whole, in all its variations over space and time and in all its relations with other systems, economic, social, political, and cultural, in the surrounding environment."[7] The dual focus on material and process in trans studies, then, certainly offers up areas of commonality for scholars of manuscript production and consumption.

Such commonalities are promising, but—to adapt a question posed in the acknowledgements of Daniel Wakelin's 2014 book *Scribal Correction and Literary Craft*—how do we know what is queer?[8] In a period where there was no alternative to the handwritten text, how do we measure queerness? To decide that everything is queer or disruptive—un*usual*, in Wakelin's words—is to decide that nothing is. Moreover, Lucy Allen-Goss points out, to do so constructs "a reverse-teleology of technologies," that associates the medieval with postmodern sensibilities and every subsequent technology with greater social restriction and normativity: an anachronistic inversion of the political nostalgia described in the previous chapter.[9] Perhaps, as Allen-Goss's observation alludes, what we are responding to is the apparent queerness of manuscript materiality when viewed from the relatively text-rich present. Compared to the uniformity and the reach of print and digital text, the manuscript appears singular, aberrant, even dissident. But this says more about our orientation toward the object (and, as shown in the previous chapter, more about manuscript studies' disciplinary orientation) than it does about the objects themselves. As Sara Ahmed explains, an object is made queer when it is not oriented towards its normative function, is dislocated or turned away from what is usual.[10] What Wakelin notices, then, when he questions our framing of what is "usual" in manuscript culture, is a need to reorient our relationship to our objects in order to identify their participation in the construction of normativity.

6 Vaccaro, "Felt Matters," 257.

7 Darnton, "What is the History of Books?" 67.

8 Wakelin, *Scribal Correction*, xi: Wakelin writes that his book was prompted by the question, "How do you know what is usual?"

9 Allen-Goss, "Technologies of Touch."

10 Ahmed, *Queer Phenomenology*, esp. 157–79.

Figure 2. A sample folio from the *Orrmulum*, ca. 1180. Oxford, Bodleian Library, MS Junius 1, fol. 91r. Courtesy of the Bodleian Library. https://digital.bodleian.ox.ac.uk/objects/90a06f70-880a-4b5b-bd30-798710afff11/, CC-BY-NC 4.0.

In fact, the majority of medieval manuscripts are highly normative—both materially and socially so. Wakelin shows, normative products are what most scribes sought, most of the time: They sought "to reproduce wording exactly, to spell conventionally, communicate unambiguously, be precise in every syllable."[11] This drive towards normativity, towards correctness, Wakelin suggests is indicative of both institutional scribal training and social investment in writing as craft. That is, expectations for the way that scribes wrote (and what they wrote about) were integrated into social life via the norm-policing institutions of the church and the state and thereby participated in the reproduction of those normative expectations. In the medieval period, then, there is such thing as handmade normativity: a normative mode that accepts and even promotes or enjoys variation within a certain set

11 Wakelin, *Scribal Correction*, 3.

of parameters. In *Immaterial Texts in Late Medieval England* (2022), Wakelin develops this idea in relation to scribal practice. For the people involved in making the book, he shows, the material quirks that accompanied the handmade text were subsidiary to their expectations of normative books. Such differences could be overlooked—holes could be patched, lines of text rerouted, bindings resewn in a myriad of contingent forms—as long as the end product did not diverge too substantially from its makers' *idea* of what a text and its status within a book should be.[12]

Of course, some manuscripts are different: experimental in form, format, or copying practice. To take an English example, the late twelfth-century manuscript of the *Orrmulum* (Figure 2)—an unfinished translation of the gospels into English made by an Augustinian canon called Orrm—is highly unconventional. Thought to be an autograph draft destined for recopying, Orrm makes use of pieces of offcut parchment that vary substantially in size. The text is written in double columns, but the writing area is not boxed or ruled and Orrm's cramped hand fills all the available space on each page. Famously, Orrm employs his own idiosyncratic (though surprisingly regular) spelling system, which introduced double consonants before every short vowel. Laura Ashe has argued that Orrm should be seen not as a marginal outlier, but as "an original thinker: a man seriously engaged with the developing theology of his time, profoundly concerned with the structures of society and community, and...focused on the needs and difficulties of laypeople." Nevertheless, Orrm's approach to these questions, she finds, "stands in precocious isolation" from other—slightly later and certainly more censorious—works of English theology.[13]

Orm's approach might set him apart from other clerical writers of his time, and his manuscript is certainly materially and linguistically non-normative (at least by the standards of what survives to us today). However, his subject matter, translations of and homilies on the Gospels, is not. The vast majority of English manuscripts that survive to us are not the English-language poetry and prose at the heart of Wakelin's books. They are Latinate liturgical manuscripts and legal documents. These manuscripts are part of an ecosystem of written material that participated in the setting and regulating of societal norms: specifically, the enforced cisheterosexuality and patrilineality of medieval church and social life. Michael Clanchy has shown that, in England after the Norman Conquest, these structures were

12 Wakelin, *Immaterial Texts*.

13 Ashe, "Originality of the *Orrmulum*," 37.

increasingly regulated through the written word. Across the twelfth and into the thirteenth century, bureaucratic writing increased at every level of society. Henry II's chancery was "capable of producing by hand hundreds of writs per week," and books on estate management recommended the keeping of lists, inventories, and records of yields to assist in the day-to-day and year-to-year management of village estates.[14] It is likely, Clanchy concludes, that by the 1300s the written word played some role in regulating the lived routines of almost everyone, whether literate or not.

Most prominently, for my purposes here, the narrativizing force of the medieval book means that on the rare occasions that a trans person—broadly conceived—enters the written record, that record is often a hostile one. That is, whether the record is literary or documentary, the trans person is there as a result of controls on, and/or to police the boundaries of, normative gender expression. In this chapter, I revisit the case of Eleanor Rykener, a trans woman picked up by authorities in London in 1395, having been caught participating in paid sex with a man named John Britby behind a market stall on a small street south of Cheapside. I analyze the way the court scribe mediates Rykener's testimony, co-opting her voice on behalf of the court in an effort to police cisheterosexist gender norms. This mediation forces us to reconsider recent scholarship focussed on reclaiming Rykener's voice as a window into medieval trans agency. However, I build on such accounts to demonstrate Rykener's tactical interactions with the legal record. In particular, her use of a performative repertoire inside and outside of the court room that reorients hostile material records in the service of gender affirmation. Rykener's practice, I suggest, presents one of a range of tactics that allowed trans people to navigate cisheterosexist power structures through the material affordances of the normative book.

In the Courtroom with Eleanor Rykener

> Undecimo die Decembris anno regni regis Ricardi secundi decimo octavo, ducti fuerunt hic coram Johanne Fressh maiore et aldermannis civitatis Londoniensis Johannes Britby de comitate Eboracum et Johannes Rykener, se Elianoram nominans veste muliebri detectus. Qui die dominica ultimo preterita per quosdam dicte civitatis ministros noctanter inter horas octavam et nonam super quoddam stallum in venella vocata Sopereslane inventi fuerunt iacentes, illud vitium detestabile, nephandum, et ignominiosum committentes.

14 Clanchy, *Memory to the Written Record*, 69 and 48–53.

> Pro seperali examinatione coram dictis maiore et aldermannis super premissa fienda et audienda etcetera. Qui quidem Johannes Britby inde allocutus fatebatur quod ipse per vicum regium de Chepe die dominica inter horas supradictas transiens, dictum Johannem Rykener vestitu muliebri ornatum, ipsumque mulierem fore suspicantem fuerat assecutus, petens ab eo, tanquam a muliere, si cum ea libidinose agere possit. Qui ab eo argentum pro labore suo petens sibi consentiebat, invicem transeuntes ad illud complendum usque stallum predictum. Ipsi tamen tunc ibidem per ministros predictos in eorum maleficiis detestabilibus capti fuerunt, carcere vero mancipati hucusque, etcetera. Et predictus Johannes Rykener in veste muliebri huc adductus de materia predicta allocutus cognovit se fecisse in omnibus prout idem Johannes Britby superius fatebatur etcetera.
>
> (On December 11, 18 Richard II, were brought in the presence of John Fresse, Mayor, and the Aldermen of the City of London John Britby of the county of York and John Rykener, calling [herself] Eleanor, having been detected in women's clothing, who were found last Sunday night between the hours of eight and nine by certain officials of the city lying by a certain stall in Soper's Lane committing that detestable, unmentionable, and ignominious vice (sodomy).
>
> In a separate examination held before the Mayor and Aldermen about the occurrence, John Britby confessed that he was passing through the high road of Cheap on Sunday between the above-mentioned hours and accosted [Eleanor] Rykener, dressed up as a woman, thinking [s]he was a woman, asking [her] as he would a woman if he could commit a libidinous act with her. Requesting money for [her] labour, Rykener consented, and they went together to the aforesaid stall to complete the act and were captured there during these detestable wrongdoings by the officials and taken to prison. And [Eleanor] Rykener, brought here in woman's clothing and questioned about this matter, acknowledged [herself] to have done everything just as John Britby had confessed.)[15]

On December 11, 1394, Eleanor Rykener and John Britby—the man who was paying her—were brought before the Mayor of the City of London, having been found the previous Sunday evening having sex by a stall on Soper's Lane. Eleanor Rykener was a queer trans woman, living and working in and around London and Oxford at the end of the fourteenth century. She is found "dressed...as a woman," "calling [herself] Eleanor," working in feminine-

15 London, The London Archives (formerly Corporation of London Records Office), Plea and Memoranda Roll A34, m. 2; see Boyd and Karras, "*Ut cum muliere*," 99–116, and Boyd and Karras, 479–85, ed. and trans. 481–85. Pronouns and names updated in square brackets in the English translation to reflect Eleanor's identity as a trans woman, paragraph breaks mine. See, also, Henningsen, "Calling [Herself] Eleanor."

coded occupations, and fulfilling the female role in sex, which she claims to have done many times in several geographic locales over a period of years. She has sex with both men and women, including clergy of both genders, both "as a man" and "as…a woman."

It is not clear why the interrogation, having to do with public sex, accusations of sodomy, and sex work taking place outside of the bounds of Southwark, was held before the civil authorities (the mayor), rather than in a canon court. It is possible, Taylor Cowdery has recently shown, that the case came to the court of the mayor of London due to the details it records about Rykener's employer, Elizabeth Brouderer, and her involvement in establishing Rykener in the sex trade. The bulk of the business that went through the mayoral court delt with mercantile and guild disputes, including the management of standards in apprenticeships. Three other disputes recorded in the Plea and Memoranda rolls for this period involved the misconduct of embroiderers and seamstresses with respect to their apprentices.[16] It is not clear that any charges were ever brought in Eleanor and John's case. If the case was passed to canon authorities, then no records have yet been identified. Perhaps the interrogation that took place at the mayoral court was enough to make an example of them.

In any case, the surviving record of the interrogation in Plea and Memoranda Roll A34, m.2 represents a rare, if heavily mediated, instance of a trans voice in the historic record. Since its rediscovery by Ruth Mazo Karras and David Boyd in 1995, Rykener's interrogation has most commonly been treated by scholars as a record of male homosexual activity and crossdressing. Gabrielle M. W. Bychowski demonstrates the cissexism (individual, disciplinary, institutional) of this approach, which assumes an historical subject to be cis unless given incontrovertible evidence to the contrary (up to and including the trans subject's own testimony).[17] Critical re-evaluation by transgender scholars has been crucial in reclaiming Eleanor's trans voice. However hostile the documentary evidence may be, Bychowski demonstrates that underlying it is a record of Rykener's own account. Rykener is attributed the verb to say (*dictus/quod*) ten times compared to Britby's two.[18] Her narrative occupies the bulk of the record and the account given of her life reaches far beyond the activities that she and Britby were picked up for on Soper Lane. Kadin Henningsen has also highlighted the importance

16 Cowdery, "Apprentice Work."

17 Bychowski, "Transgender Turn," esp. 99–105.

18 Boyd and Karras, "Interrogation," 481–82.

of Rykener's voice: by "calling [herself] Eleanor" in this context, he notes, Rykener has "strategically—and perhaps even defiantly—*inscribe[d]* herself into the historical record as a woman."[19] Both scholars reinforce their claims for Rykener's agency in the account by drawing attention to further examples. For instance, she takes on gendered labour, as an embroiderer, a tapster (a barmaid), and a sex worker: all feminine-coded jobs. She dresses herself "in women's clothing." And, when Britby propositions her, Rykener "turn[s] in response," negotiating payment (*argentum*) for her labour (*labore*) before she will consent (*consentum*) to the encounter. Bychoswki figures these actions in terms of the "transgender turn," which she defines as a "turn[ing] out toward and speak[ing] back to cisgender people and cisgender versions of history."[20] Rykener's negotiation with Britby constitutes a turning back of cis assumptions and power dynamics. Through these actions, Rykener demonstrates her power within the relationship—to consent or not, to seek payment for her labour or not—and her position as a collaborator rather than a sexual object.[21]

Other people also participate in validating Rykener's trans experience. Henningsen employs Jane Ward's theory of "gender labor"—"the affective and bodily efforts invested in giving gender to others…the work of bolstering someone's gender authenticity"—to explain how other people in the record participate in Rykener's gender construction.[22] Two women, Elizabeth Brouderer and Anna, taught Rykener how to dress and have sex "in the manner of a woman"; Elizabeth was also the first to call Rykener Eleanor; John Clerk of the Swan Inn employed Rykener as a tapster; and multiple people are named as having sexual intercourse with her "as a woman."[23] These events map variously onto the gendered and gender labour that Henningsen describes, which include the labour of alliance (Brouderer, Anna, John Clerk), the labour of forgetting, and the labour of being "the man" (Rykener's clients). For example, the account opens with John Britby's description of his encounter with Rykener. His multiple assertions that he perceived Rykener was a woman, and approached her as a woman, and spoke to her "as he would a woman," accompanied by his use of the feminine pronoun "ea," help to foreground Rykener's status as "*the* woman" in their interaction. As a presumed cis man, "Britby

19 Henningsen, "Calling [Herself] Eleanor," 251, emphasis mine.

20 Bychowski, "Transgender Turn," 98.

21 Bychowski, "Transgender Turn," 110.

22 Henningsen, "Calling [Herself] Eleanor," 257; see Ward, "Gender Labor," 237.

23 Boyd and Karras, "Interrogation," 483.

supports Eleanor's identity as a woman through 'surface reinforcements' such as pronouns and calling her Eleanor, as well as the 'more complex work of actually participating in the production of [his] partner's gender (through sex acts and roles, through shared gender dynamics, and through the private work of thinking and/or feeling sexual orientation in connection with [her] gender identity).'"[24]

The preservation of Rykener's voice—not only in the reports of her testimony (*quod/dicus*), but also in her negotiations with Britby, her agreement on location, and her granting of consent—and the agency she displays in her self-presentation, has led scholars to frame her as a co-author of the documentary record, shaping her testimony as an act of ongoing self-fashioning.[25] This document is, as Bychowski puts it, "first and foremost a record produced about and by Rykener."[26] Recovering Rykener's voice is crucial as a means of "reckoning" with the cissexism of the historical establishment—which insisted on reading Rykener as a homosexual man—and of the record itself, constructed and controlled by the cis men who accused her.[27] I am grateful for the work of trans scholars who have taken steps to reclaim Eleanor Rykener's voice from the historical record. I appreciate the significance of such efforts to cross-temporal coalition building, validating trans existence in the face of current political claims of "novelty,"[28] and critiquing the construction of cis hegemonies. It is not my intention to undermine such efforts, but to reinforce them—as a book historian—with an interrogation of the role of the material record. However, we cannot let the promise of hearing Rykener speak elide or obscure the reality of cissexism. This record is a hostile one, as are most interactions trans people have had with historical documentation, and alongside celebrating the vivid life that it recalls we should be conscious that it documents an unpleasant and possibly traumatic experience and an attempt to suppress Rykener's humanity.

---

24 Henningsen, "Calling [Herself] Eleanor," 261, quoting Chess, *Male-to-Female Crossdressing*, 140.

25 Bychowski, "Transgender Turn," 109–10; Henningsen, "Calling [Herself] Eleanor," 251.

26 Bychowski, "Transgender Turn," 106.

27 Bychowski, "Transgender Turn," 110.

28 That is, the idea that trans identities are "new" and thus somehow invalid and evidence of a kind of "social contagion" that must be eradicated: for more, see Heyam, *Before We Were Trans*, 22–26.

Voicing the Hostile Archive

Any voice that Rykener is given in Plea and Memoranda Roll A34 has been heavily mediated by the scribe and the documentary conventions of the (cishetero) legal establishment. Naming Rykener as co-author of the record recognizes the work of self-fashioning it documents, but elides the attempted suppression of Rykener's choice, voice, and ability to self-define. We see these attempts in—among other features—the scribe's privileging of Britby's account over Rykener's; in his unquestioned sexualization of her and, by extension, all women ("as he would a woman"); and in the scribe's (almost) consistent misnaming and misgendering of her.[29] It is important that we do not overstate Rykener's power in this legal situation, and thereby make her complicit in her own subjugation.

According to Judith Butler, gender is *performative*. It is constructed through the deployment of self-constituting performative *speech acts*. That is, rather than describing an observable phenomenon (a *constative* speech act, e.g., "The apple is red"), the speech acts that produce gender do "not need a material referent to be meaningful," are not measurable, and create the conditions they describe through the act of "doing."[30] Butler gives the example of wedding vows ("I do"), which are abstract in themselves, but when said by the appropriate people (prospective spouses) in the appropriate context (a marriage ceremony) create the condition of being married.[31] Butler demonstrates that gender operates through similar structures. However, unlike the act of marriage, gender must be constantly—and ideally for cis hegemony, consistently—re-enacted, both as a marker of individual identity and in support of the binary gender system. The act of naming is one such performative act: names are not innate or meaningful in themselves, they are chosen (usually by a parent around the time we are born) and become synonymous with one's personhood only through consistent and repeated use. In the UK, the process for changing a name is reflective of the performative nature of the act. All that is needed is a statutory declaration, in which one states that they "absolutely and entirely renounce, relinquish and abandon the use of" the former name

29 See Bychowski, "Transgender Turn," 103–5 for a more expansive unpacking of the cissexism of the historical record.

30 Stryker, "(De)Subjugated Knowledges," 10, with reference to Butler, *Gender Trouble*; Butler, *Bodies that Matter*.

31 See Butler, *Bodies that Matter*, 170.

and "assume, adopt and determine to take and use" the new name.[32] Crucially, it is the continued and consistent use of the name that makes the declaration meaningful. So, in "calling [herself]" by a feminine-coded name, and in having others do so also, Rykener participates in the performative structures of womanhood.

However, it would be hard to argue for the performative success of Rykener's speech as it is described in Plea and Memoranda Roll A34. Rykener's claims to femininity are narrated by the scribe as a representative of the legal system. First, her words are in the legal Latin of court documentary culture, rather than provided in the English that she probably spoke.[33] Her speech is narrated in the third person ("[She] further said"), replicates documentary linguistic structures that refer to both the commonplaces of the genre and the form of the document ("the above said," "confessed," "exercise this vice," "etcetera"), and fixates on and repeats details of time, place, and person ("for how long and in what places and with what persons") as directed by the interrogation.[34] The scribe consistently misnames and misgenders Eleanor (thirteen of the pronouns used by the scribe are male), with the reflexive construction "se Elianoram nominans (calling [herself] Eleanor)" suggestive of a lack of agreement between Eleanor's own statement and the perception of others.

Most crucially, in the context it is deployed here—i.e., by the scribe in response to an interrogation after an arrest related to sodomy, prostitution, and gender non-conformity—the narrativized speech no longer functions to assert Rykener's gender, but to deconstruct or delegitimize it. While the image of Rykener unapologetically telling her story may resonate with a sympathetic audience, this document is designed to witness her failure to satisfactorily perform cisheterosexuality. By denying her womanhood (through the co-opting of her voice), the record suggests she has not succeeded in occupying the feminine role, despite providing details of multiple instances in which she does so. This is not to say that Rykener's agency is not to be found, or that she had not successfully inhabited her gender up to this point. But, I suggest the invocation of her speech in this context serves a particular ideological purpose: to position her transness as a lie to which she can only confess ("item fatebatur ([She] further confessed)"), and so to

32 This formulation comes directly from the wording of my own, legally binding, statutory declaration.

33 See Clanchy, *Memory to the Written Record*, 209–11.

34 Boyd and Karras, "Interrogation," 483.

deconstitute her gender and bring it back in line with cissexist standards. Rykener's agency is found where her actions assume a purpose unintended by the scribe (and the institution) reporting her words.

Performative Repertoire as Trans Tactic

In Isaac West's account of the arrest and trial of Debbie Mayne, a trans woman engaged in sex work in and around Pershing Square, Los Angeles in 1955, he documents Mayne's tactics for intervening into the legal record. In Mayne's case, this begins with her decision to get arrested in the first place, which she did on two occasions, both times by approaching a police office and declaring she had entered gendered spaces counter to her sex. The first incident occurred on November 14, when Mayne entered the men's public bathroom dressed as a man. Upon exiting she approached the officer, who she knew, and declared that she had undergone sex-reassignment surgery and intended to present as a woman. She was arrested for "masquerading as a man." On December 6 she returned to Pershing Square and used the women's bathroom. Afterwards she again approached the officer and was then arrested for "masquerading as a woman" and "outraging public decency."[35] Mayne's intention in provoking these arrests seems to have been to make her gender a matter of public record and set a precedent for trans recognition under the law. However, the judge who heard her cases (which the prosecutor combined into one hearing), "side stepped the issue of Mayne's legal sex, choosing instead to focus on" the charge of "masquerade." As a result, Mayne's voice and her intention are stripped out of her interaction with the legal record. The documents seem to "offer[...] little more than fragmentary evidence of the legal problems of one transsexual in a historically specific moment."[36]

One object of West's research into Mayne is to challenge the value of visibility as an outcome of scholarly inquiry. Visibility, he suggests, construed broadly as the materials that make it into the public record for others to see, masks the "dynamic operations of domination and resistance" that shape the legal system. In other words, for trans people, the legal record, as it acts as a record of presence, is already skewed toward oppression—Rykener's voice has already been co-opted by the legal establishment. A focus on visibility, West suggests, citing James Scott, elides "the immense political terrain

35 West, "Mayne's Trans/scripts," 245–46. Debbie Mayne is a pseudonym first used by Meyerowitz, *How Sex Changed*. Archival records related to Mayne are kept at the Kinsey Institute for Research in Sex, Gender, and Reproduction.

36 West, "Mayne's Trans/scripts," 246.

that lies between quiescence and revolt" and the small acts of agency, resistance, and resilience that inhabit it and undergird what happens in the court room.[37] Mayne, West observes, did not broach any new legal or medical ground as a result of her interactions with the State, nor did she acquire much long-term celebrity, so the frame of *visibility*, of noticing her presence, functions primarily to extend a very limited list of historic trans people who enter the legal record and provides little information on the richness, complexity, and extent of trans lives.

As a means of moving beyond the invocation of voice as a measure of visibility and an exertion of power within the written record, West employs the model of "performative repertoires." The term "performative repertoire" describes the suite of tactics that Mayne used to develop and practice agency outside of the moment of legal record and thereby "traverse[...] the discursive circuitries available to her" and circumvent the appropriation of the court.[38] Mayne's repertoires take the form of "embodied practices," which are used to navigate "logics of recognition and domination" and provide "psychic spaces of resistance." Practices like provoking her own arrest(s): "Mayne did not wait for the law to find her; rather, by seeking out a confrontation with the law, she pre-empted her inevitable interpellation as a sexual deviant and criminal."[39] West constructs the performative repertoire, as a corollary to Butler's explanation of constrained agency. "The one who acts," Butler observes, "acts precisely to the extent that he or she is constituted as an actor, and, hence, operat[es] within a linguistic field of enabling constraints from the outset."[40] When speech is constrained or circumscribed by the legal establishment, performative repertoires present a tactic for generating "alternative articulatory pathways in the circuitries of power."[41]

West looks for such tactics within the "hidden transcripts" of Mayne's personal correspondence and medical record, which he contrasts to the public legal record and press articles. Here he observes her varied communication registers, the way she presents herself within a range of interpersonal scenarios, and other embodied modes of information transmission. These techniques allow Mayne to move beyond the limits placed upon her by the mediating form of the cis legal establishment and its records, which control

37 West, "Mayne's Trans/scripts," 246–47, citing Scott, *Arts of Resistance*, 140.

38 West, "Mayne's Trans/scripts," 256.

39 West, "Mayne's Trans/scripts," 247.

40 Butler, *Excitable Speech*, 16.

41 West, "Mayne's Trans/scripts," 250.

how she may be categorized, controlled, and historicized. West figures these "quotidian practices as important sites of identity creation, agency, and politics."[42] Here, performative repertoires provide tactics of trans resistance to the subjugation enacted by the normative documents of the legal record, "strategic critical resource[s] in resisting the expansion and sedimentation of legal hegemonies."[43] In so doing, they refuse the courtroom record, drawing in the gestures, expressions, and relationships of a life outside.

For Rykener, no records exist beyond Plea and Memoranda Roll A34, but Henningsen's analysis of the gendered and gender labour exerted by Rykener and her peers provides a starting point for assessing the performative repertoires that she employs outside of this record. In fact, the record provided by Plea and Memoranda Roll A34 is often pointing outward. Rykener references her travel between places—London, Oxford, Burford, and Beaconsfield—and her relationships with people—Elizabeth Brouderer, Anna, John Clerk, Sir William Foxlee, Brother Michael, and Joan Matthew—who assist in her passage, employment, and self-presentation. Like Mayne, we might suppose that she communicated with these people in different registers, with different objectives in mind. Rykener and Brouderer, for instance, seem to have shared an intimate and caring relationship: Rykener was dressed by Brouderer, was familiar with her daughter, was named by her, and on at least one occasion met with a client in Brouderer's house. "[G]ender labor," by Ward's definition, "is the act of giving gender to others," which comprises of the "intimate" duties of "witnessing, nurturing, validating, fulfilling, authenticating, special knowing, and secret-keeping."[44] According to Rykener's account, Anna (a sex worker associated with a former servant of Thomas Blount) and Elizabeth Brouderer instigated many firsts (*primo/prius*) in her gender journey, "giving" Rykener gender through naming, dressing, and teaching her to "be 'the girl.'"[45]

In taking on feminine-coded work (gender*ed* labour)—not only sex work, but piece work as a seamstress and a tapster—Rykener takes on a culturally recognizable form of female embodiment that would register in the spaces she occupied, the objects she used, and activities she undertook. Her clothing stakes similar claims to culturally sanctioned femininity, and her choice of what to wear, when, and how, as guided by Brouderer, stages a series of negotiations that implicate various forms of embodied cultural

---

42 West, "Mayne's Trans/scripts," 256.

43 West, "Mayne's Trans/scripts," 249.

44 Ward, "Gender Labor," 240.

45 See Ward, "Gender Labor," 242.

knowledge. We do not know, for example, whether there were certain fashion choices that signalled her willingness to undertake sex work to John Britby. We do know that, after having sex with Phillip, the rector of Theydon Garnon, at Brouderer's house, Rykener "took away two gowns (*togas*)" belonging to Philip. When Philip attempted to negotiate the return of the gowns, Rykener "said that [she] was the wife of a certain man and that if Philip wished to ask for them back [she] would make [her] husband bring suit against him."[46] Here, Rykener takes on the role—voice, presentation, embodiment, entitlement—of the wronged wife of a powerful man in convincing enough style to warn Philip off. We might imagine the "kind of person" who would make such a threat and see Rykener affecting the Karen-esque bearing required to carry it off.

The performance of these embodied social repertoires afforded Rykener modes of resistance that slip the bounds of mediated text and allow us to see past it to other claims of agency. Sometimes those claims enter the courtroom. Having been "detected in women's clothing" at her arrest, it might be considered prudent if, when Rykener appeared for interrogation, she dressed to comply with the legal establishment's preferences. Instead, she is presented "in woman's clothing."[47] While her choice might be dictated by many considerations and contingencies—was Rykener held in custody or released between arrest and questioning? Was she provided with alternative clothing? Was presenting as feminine an attempt to subvert the charges of sodomy laid against them?—they visibly bring the transfeminine performative repertoire Rykener employs in other aspects of her life into the courtroom in a way that resists the standards the state operates through and the subjugation it enacts.

When faced with a courtroom full of hostile witnesses, Rykener had a range of options available to her. She could have clammed up, given minimal or evasive answers, or denied any further involvement than the sex that she and Britby were engaged in when they were caught. Instead, her testimony is extensive. In sharing the details of her social roles, the multiple feminine registers they occupy, and invoking the gender labour of others to sustain them, she enters her gender into a cissexist record than cannot and will not recognize or give credit to her voice. This decision, made knowingly or not, presents a tactic of resistance. Rykener retains her agency over her presentation, even as her words are co-opted through the workings of the written record.

---

46 Boyd and Karras, "Interrogation," 483.

47 Boyd and Karras, "Interrogation," 483.

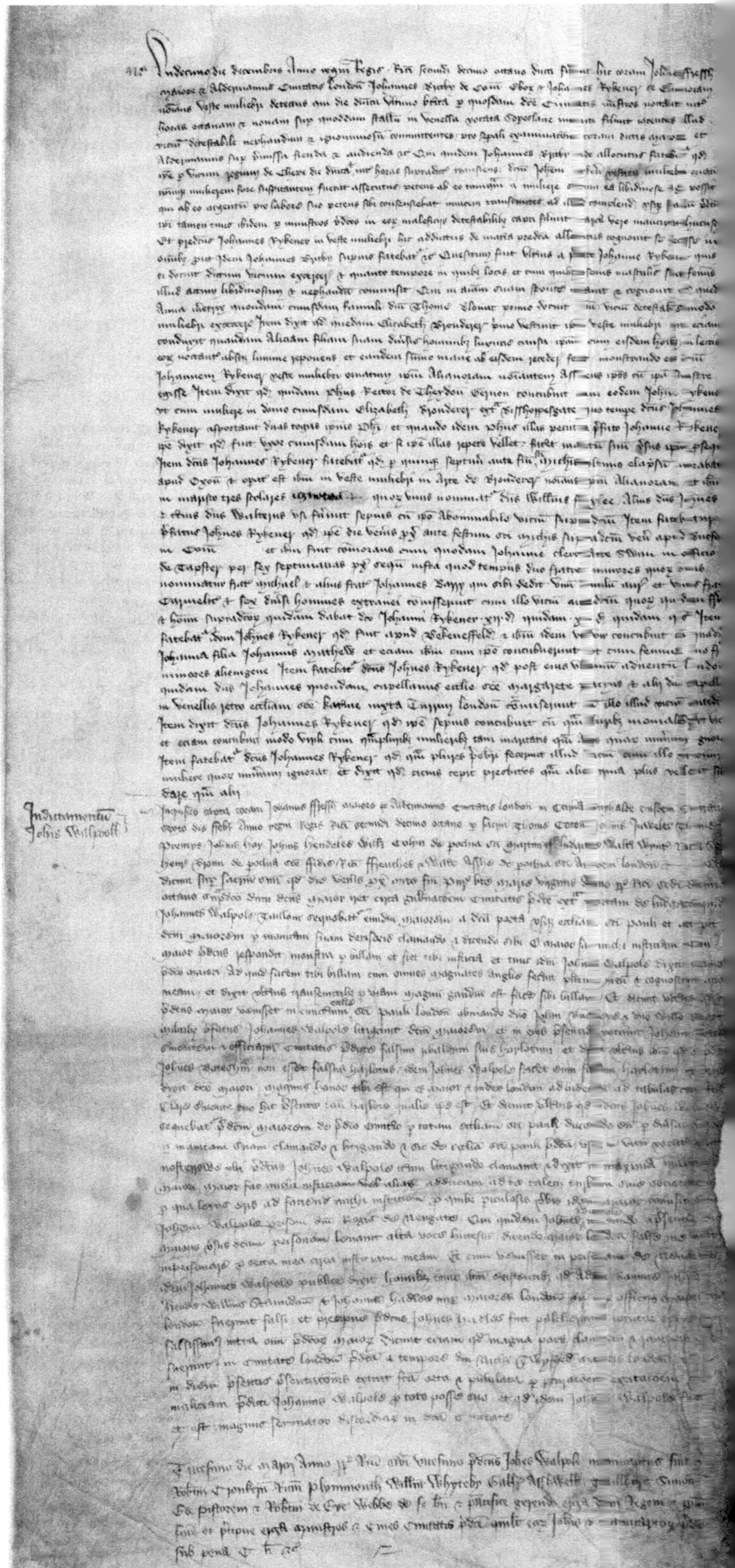

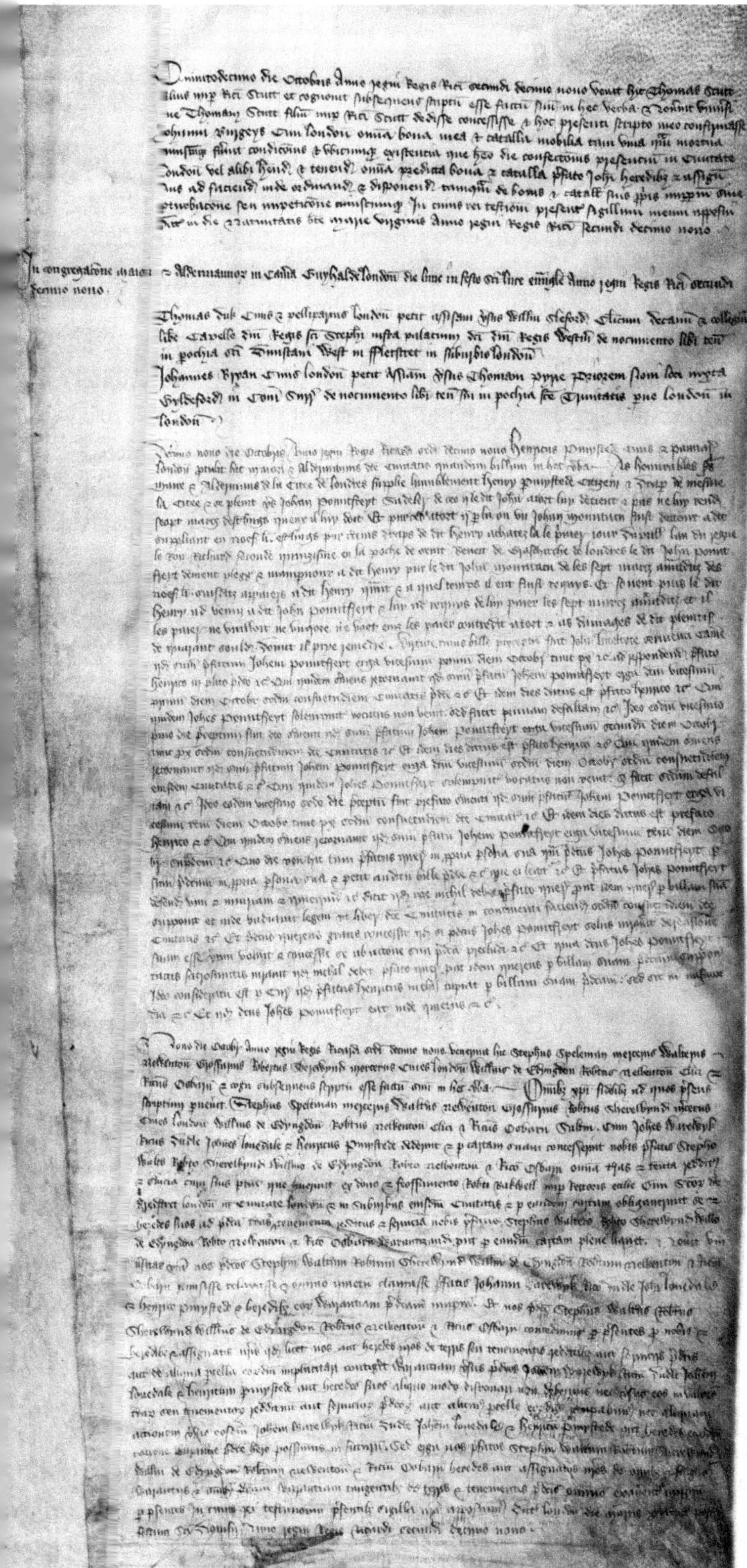

Figure 3. Record of the interrogation of Eleanor Rykener in its manuscript context, 1394. London, The London Archives (formerly Corporation of London Records Office), Plea and Memoranda Roll A34, m. 2r and v. Reproduced by permission of The London Archives.

Material Tactics for the Normative Record

Revisiting the formulations used by Henningsen and Bychowski to describe Rykener's agency over the text refocuses attention on the materiality of the document. The terms "inscrib[ing]" and "co-author[ing]" highlight the document's status as written record, both the product of embodied labour and a claim to material longevity.[48] *Inscription*, in particular, conjures images of permanence, memorialization in stone, and in one sense of the Latin verb (*inscribo*) branding on skin.[49] While Plea and Memoranda Roll A34 may be a hostile document, founded on the principal of ensuring conformity with cisheterosexist social and legal expectations, can we see the record of Rykener's embodied performative repertoires that it sustains as a redeployment of the document's material qualities for legitimizing purposes? I suggest that the repertoires indicated by Rykener's testimony, and that give her agency by extending her narrative beyond the subjugated setting of the courtroom, can be extended to—even come to a head in—her use of the record itself.

My claim rests on several observations about the document (Figure 3). First, that the plea and memoranda rolls of the Corporation of London were produced to record pleas and sometimes cases of those called before the mayor's, Staple, and mercantile courts in perpetuity, and took the form of running rolls sometimes spanning several calendar years. The roll on which Rykener's questioning is recorded reports cases from the mayor's court, beginning on November 4, 1394 and running to July 4, 1395—it spans three membranes (recto and dorse), Rykener's case is on membrane 2r. In this material context, the roll is not a working document to be used in the courtroom or in the calculation of duties, but a best copy designed—in theory—to be the object of historical record and given orderly place within the chronology of the workings of the court.[50] The plea and memoranda rolls of this

---

48 Henningsen, "Calling [Herself] Eleanor," 251, and Bychowski, "Transgender Turn," 110 respectively.

49 Lewis and Short, *Latin Dictionary*, *inscribo*, sense II.B.3.

50 In practice, the survival of the Mayor's Court rolls is sporadic compared to those of the other courts of the Guildhall: on several occasions steps were taken by the city aldermen to encourage the four attorneys of the Mayoral Court to keep their records in the Chamber or in the City Treasury, suggesting that often those records were taken to or kept in private houses. It is also possible that the mayor, like the sheriff, retained at least some of his documents after he retired from office, in case he needed to defend himself against an appeal. The selective use of the plea and memoranda rolls in the late fourteenth century might be the result of scribes copying only what was pertinent from these longer documents before they were released to the mayor.

period contain only the records of the mayor's court that "seemed to the clerks worthy of remembrance either as legal precedents or as illustrations of the rights, privileges, and pre-eminence of the City."[51] The 1394–1395 plea and memoranda rolls, then, unlike the original rolls and other documents of court proceedings, present a curated history of the business of the year. The selection of records included lay out the priorities and values of the court as they reflect those of the wider political establishment—in Rykener's case, the reinforcement of compulsory cisheterosexuality—and assert them as historical truth.

Although the case is longer than some of the other items in the roll, the record of Rykener's questioning conforms visually with the institutional standards of the surrounding entries (compare Figure 3, right). The text is copied as a solid orderly block, in a mixed cursive hand akin to many others used by the scribes of the Guildhall. The Latin is lightly abbreviated, as you might expect of a best copy. The record begins with a note in the margin, marking the start of a new item. The first initial is slightly larger, with some flourishing, and some other majuscules on the top line are extended, but the script overall maintains an even ductus and size throughout. Such features work alongside the institutional context of its production to reproduce the authority of the court across time. They situate Rykener's case within normative documentary standards, in an effort to craft a record that forces institutional conformity.

Debbie Mayne demonstrates, in her correspondence, a repeated concern that her trial was being used as a "test case," with the result that it had a national audience: "This decision," she wrote, "will effect every case in the Country."[52] In her performative repertoire, as it appears in her "hidden transcripts," West identifies Mayne's active engagement with the legal system and selective deployment of information within the courtroom as a tactic of resistance, an attempt to force legal gender recognition by activating the court's normativizing documentary standards and to build on that recognition among a wider social milieu. Crucially, what Mayne wanted out of this interaction was not a radical departure from normative models. Rather, Mayne wanted incorporation into normative institutional modes; as she expressed it, to "get her operations" and to go about her business without

---

There was also substantial loss of Guildhall documents in the Great Fire of London: Thomas, ed., *Early Mayor's Court Rolls*, vii–viii.

51 *Early Mayor's Court Rolls*, ed. Thomas, vii.

52 West, "Mayne's Trans/scripts," 255.

harassment from the police.[53] Eleanor Rykener's performative repertoire, as expressed in her courtroom testimony, shows (at least in part) a similar drive towards some kinds of normative gender expression. Her participation in feminine-coded work, dress, naming, and relationships represents a taking on of normative—if marginalized—types of womanhood. In choosing to deploy the evidence of these repertoires in the courtroom, Rykener may show an equal awareness of the historicizing and normativizing role of the documentary record. These records were not intended for public consumption, but they were invested in curating a version of the "truth," and the presence of Rykener's testimony within this standardized form, extends this version of truth to the performative gender repertoires she deployed in the courtroom.

Second, I suggest that Rykener's tactical use of the normative record is enhanced by its status as a handwritten document. Such records, despite their standardization, rest on the embodied labour of the scribe and all the contingencies that come with that. Just as Rykener's testimony might be coopted (as "confession") for cissexist legal purposes, the scribe's embodied labour was susceptible to being subverted and redeployed. As we will see in the next chapter, in handwritten texts, scribal intention is easily redirected, recruited, or collapsed. The reader (and the editor) looks through the work of the scribe toward another, more authoritative, more authorial, voice. This truism is registered by those scholars that have looked to this text as evidence of Rykener's speech. Scribes themselves are fallible, and corrections, like the one apparent in the centre of the record, are more easily and less traceably applied than they would be in paper and print. While Rykener did not have control over the reproduction and redeployment of her voice in the legal record, she could use her curation and presentation of material, including a full and flexible range of performative gender repertoires, as a means of claiming the tools of historicization (and thereby "truth"). Her courtroom performance may not save her speech from the cisheterosexist establishment, but the material record is subject to its own contingencies and the embodied repertoires her testimony calls out to are less easily overwritten. In fact, the materiality of the document affords both the historicization and reclamation of Rykener's trans experience.

53 West, "Mayne's Trans/scripts," 252.

Chapter 3

MANUSCRIPT KINSHIP AND FAMILY TREES

STEMMATICS—THE PROCESS TRADITIONALLY used by manuscript scholars to decide which variants to present in an edition—is based on the model of genealogical descent. The German philologist Karl Lachmann is generally attributed with the systemization of the stemmatic method, by which manuscript variants across a textual tradition are compared in order to establish related groupings and probable lines of descent from a hypothetical error-free authorial original. Critiques of the method, and the recensionist editorial practices derived from it, have perpetuated since its earliest development, resulting in various procedural and objective-based adjustments.

The stemmatic approach has been subject to two major and overlapping critiques. The first, mainly coming from editors and book historians working within the discipline of manuscript studies, is that the method does not reflect the material realities of manuscript transmission. I expand on Michael Sargent's suggestion that stemmatics rests on two false principles: the "principle of overdetermination (that although a given manuscript in a complex pattern of diffusion may demonstrate a number of conflicting agreements in common variation with various other manuscripts, it must be assigned a single location in the textual pedigree); and the principle of false Ockhamism (that the smallest number of branches of diffusion must be the most probable)."[1] As scholars have struggled to reprioritize various features of individual manuscripts alongside the text a growing separation has appeared between the material analysis of manuscripts and the way that we map their textual relations. Other models have been proposed to understand scribal copying practices and modes of manuscript transmission. New Philology, Stephen Nicols writes in his seminal introduction to *Speculum*'s 1990 special issue on the subject, suggests that "[r]ecalling that almost all manuscripts postdate the life of the author by decades or even centuries, one recognizes the manuscript matrix as a place of radical contingencies:

1 Sargent, "Organic and Cybernetic Metaphors," 212.

of chronology, of anachronism, of conflicting subjects, of representation."[2] However, stemmatics continues to visualize textual relations as static chronological and genealogical systems.

Second, feminist scholars reject the language and rhetoric of stemmatics for the cisheteropatriarchal limitations it sets on the field of inquiry. "A rhetoric of heteronormativity, repronormativity, and patrilineality more specifically is deployed to group manuscripts into 'families' of originals and derivatives," observe Roberta Magnani and Diane Watt, "these derivatives are, in turn, chastised for their inferior and corrupt status which removes them further away from the fetishized authorial original." Per Chapter 1, we might remember that the concerns of the cisheteropatriarchy are also racially inflected. Compare, for instance, the language of corruption used by the antiquary and editor, Joseph Ritson (1752–1803)—a representation of the nationalist philological impulse of the time—, "[t]he Saxon language, after having been corrupted by the Danes, who spoke a tongue of distant affinity, began to be infected, by the Norman-French."[3] Infection follows corruption as changes to the Old English language belie the untenable fantasy of white Anglo-Saxonism. The "patriarchal paradigms" that Magnani and Watt observe, lead to value-laden judgments and what texts deserve academic remembrance, and which manuscripts might be of scholarly import. They act as barriers to inclusion—shaping the demographics of the field by signalling who is welcome and who is not. But they also fail to account for the vicissitudes of much medieval authorship, which often involved elements of compilation, collaboration, and anonymity not transposable onto the idea of masculinist authorship that these models project and reinforce.

This chapter questions, as others have done before, the patrilineal logic that governs models based on genetic filiation. I take up Sargent's suggestion for a rhizomic model of manuscript relations in order to think more widely about non-linear transmission, with the conclusion that individual abruptions and evolutions of transmission—like the abruption of queer being—provide better models than the cishetero nuclear family for understanding the medieval reading experience. I take seriously the proposition that Gilles Deleuze and Félix Guattari's rhizome, and the queer and trans familial politics it has been applied to, provides a different perspective on the relationships governing manuscript production. In doing so, I engage with both of the critiques presented above and demonstrate their enmeshment in a

2 Nichols, "Philology," 8.

3 Ritson, ed., *Romanceës*, lxii.

shared cisheteropatriarchal logic. Finally, I turn to constellation, used by V. Jo Hsu to formulate relations between literatures that might offer a home to queer and trans Asian Americans. Trans approaches to relationality and kinship, through the rhizome and the constellation, I suggest, present other ways of thinking about manuscript relations that emphasize contingency, counteractivity, cross pollination, and disrupt the teleological drive towards cultural modernity.

The Family Tree

> It is important to consider how compulsory heterosexuality—defined as the accumulative effect of the repetition of the narrative of heterosexuality as an ideal coupling—shapes what it is possible for bodies to do, even if it does not contain what it is possible to be. Bodies take the shape of norms that are repeated over time and with force.
>
> Ahmed, *The Cultural Politics of Emotion*, 145.

Lachmannean stemmatics posits that, by comparing scribal variants across a textual tradition, it is possible to understand the manuscripts of that tradition as related families of objects. Karl Lachmann (1793–1851) developed his model as both response to and support for the creation of critical editions: stemmatic modelling is based on the comparison of manuscript variants, and its outcomes help scholars and editors decide which readings to privilege and which to amend in the quest for the urtext. This method became known as the "common-error method," "according to which it is unlikely that two scribes will make the exact same error in the same place independently. Thus two or more witnesses that transmit the same error most likely derived the faulty reading from a common ancestor."[4] The resultant relationship diagrams take the form of family trees that map the descent of manuscript witnesses from a single originary source through bipartite divergences from that source (Figure 4).[5] For textual critics, the common-error method was codified into the editorial practice known as recension. In the intervening period, scholars have become less convinced by the hunt for an authorial original, but many of the mid twentieth-century editions medievalists rely on are based on recensionist practice (albeit with its objectives altered to focus on establishing a best text or archetype of a tradition.)

4 Greir, "Lachmann," 271.

5 For a more substantial overview of this history, see Sargent, "Organic and Cybernetic Metaphors," 199–208.

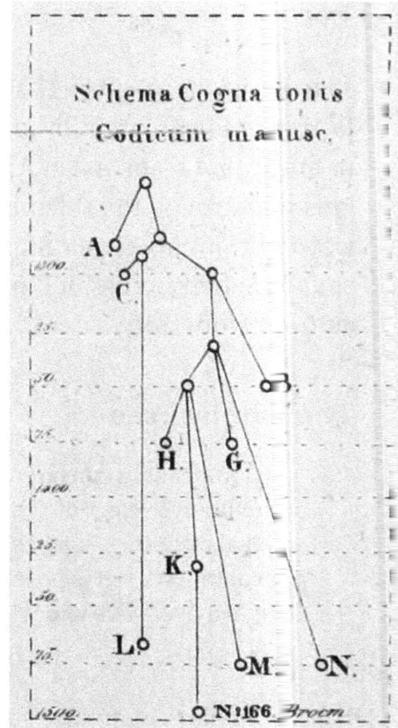

Figure 4. The earliest known stemma made for a textual tradition. "Schema Cognationis Codicum Manuscriptum," in Carl Johan Schlyter and Hans Samuel Collin, eds. *Corpus iuris Sueo-Gotorum antiqui*, Samling af Sweriges Gamla lagar, vol. 1. (Häggström, 1827), table 3. Internet Archive.

Moreover, the dramatic increase in computer power over the last generation has marked a return to recension in digital editing projects based on phylogenetic models.

Generations of editors and textual critics have pointed to the anachronisms in Lachmann's methods. Scribes did more than just introduce error to their texts. Matthew Fisher and others have noted the editorial, sometimes authorial, role taken by some scribes, who took pains to update, amend, and improve aspects of the copy text that they found wanting.[6] Meanwhile, Daniel Wakelin has emphasized the effort made by most scribes to copy correctly, which might include correcting areas of the exemplar where error was perceived.[7] Scribal variation, these scholars show, is neither the inevitable product of lazy rote copyists, nor a unidirectional journey away from a platonic textual ideal. Rather, it derives from the material and lived experiences of individual copyists. Variation is a wide-ranging category that might include mistakes, but could also incorporate creative intervention, editing, critical comparison, cross-referencing, and attempts at correction. Moreover, particular words, texts, or material contexts might invite identical variants from different scribes working at unrelated points in the textual tradition, or a scribe may detect and remedy error in an exemplar so that the resultant copy is cleaner than the one before it.

Suggestions to the contrary are characterized by moralizing and pathologizing language indicative of the white supremacist and cisheteropatriarchal standards under which these methods developed. So, when editors like Sir George Warner (1845–1936) describe a group of variant manuscripts of *The Book of John Mandeville* as "defective," Tom White finds, his use of that word is "underwritten by the essentializing pseudoscientific abstractions

6 Fisher, *Scribal Authorship*.

7 Wakelin, *Scribal Correction*, 55.

of Social Darwinism. Textual bibliography and Social Darwinism," White observes, "shared a deep disciplinary and ideological investment in the elaboration of hierarchies and genealogies, and in the construction of a national corpus purged, as far as was practicable, of its 'defective' elements."[8] Warner's work, like that of many of his contemporaries treated in Chapter 1, was heavily imbricated in contemporary colonialism. He edited the text for The Roxburghe Club, an elite literary society with membership limited to forty, mostly imperial politicians and members of the landed aristocracy, and—White has shown— "Warner cannot help but see his *Book* as a precursor to British imperialism."[9] Warner's use of the term "defective" invokes the late nineteenth-century language of disability, and with it (according to contemporary pseudo-science) the heritable features of race.[10] The language, of course, is dehumanizing, both to the scribes who produced these variant manuscripts, and to modern readers and users. It has also limited scholarly attention to this larger group of manuscripts, preventing proper engagement with the variation that they have with one another on the basis of one perceived commonality.[11]

All this before we get to the thorny category of premodern authorship. Medieval "authors" engaged in a range of activities—translation, collation, compilation—alongside freeform composition. Medieval literature is, as Bernard Cerquiglini puts it, "a literature that is in conflict with that authenticity and uniqueness that textuary thought connects with aesthetic production."[12] Moreover, some authors refashioned their texts, sometimes after the first copies had been made. William Langland undertook three significant revisions of *Piers Plowman*, resulting in three dramatically different traditions now known as the A, B, and C-text. However, some of the scribes who worked on its manuscripts, clearly came into contact with exemplars from more than one of those textual traditions. Rather than choose between the traditions he encountered, Richard Osbarn, the fifteenth-century scribe of Huntington Library, MS HM 114 (or the redactor of another manuscript earlier its copying history) sought to harmonize the work by interpolating

---

8 White, "National Philology," 832. See also, Grigely, *Textualterity*, esp. 19–30, which charts a different course through the connections between eugenics and philological method than I did in Chapter 1.

9 White, "National Philology," 840.

10 White, "National Philology," 841–45.

11 White, "National Philology," 846.

12 Cerquiglini, *In Praise of the Variant*, 33.

sections of A and C into his copy of the B-text.[13] The result is a hybrid text. At least four exempla went into the making of the material that ended up as the text of HM 114, including two copies of the C-text (one potentially integrated into the A-text prologue and one independent).[14] It is impossible, therefore, to relate the manuscript neatly to any one of the three family groups: integrating it into stemmatic representations requires that it appear more than once, or begin a new family of its own. As a result, editors have rejected the manuscript as "ruinously corrupt." George Kane and E. Talbot Donaldson excluded the variants it preserves from their edition of the B-text, as including them would "more than doubled the size of the critical apparatus."[15]

The arboriform stemma, which replicates the form of the cisheteró family tree (Figure 4), belies its patrilineal investments, visually privileging the original over all other copies.[16] Like the search for the urtext, this investment partly stems from the valorization of the author as sole originary force. In such models, all manuscripts (worth knowing) are the progeny of a white male author, whose existence forms the basis of their authority and assures them a place in the canon. Conversely, each generation of remove from the author represents a step away from the ideal of the original. The resultant model, therefore, engages in what Elizabeth Freeman calls, the "chronopolitics of development."[17] It is at once regressive, in its search for the mythologized original, and positivist, in its teleological ambition to plot change over time. The chronopolitics of development describes the ideological conditions that prompt "supposedly post-imperial states" to "track and manage their own denizens through an official time line, effectively shaping the contours of a meaningful life by registering some events like birth, marriages, deaths, and refusing to record others like initiations, friendships, and contact with the dead."[18] Such chrononormative moments (and their registra-

---

13 San Marino, Huntington Library, MS HM 114 (*Piers Plowman*). See Wood, "Nonauthorial *Piers*"; Bart, "Intellect, Influence." For a full account of the interpolations see Russell and Nathan, "*Piers Plowman* Manuscript." For the scribal identification, Mooney and Stubbs, *Scribes in the City*, 17–37.

14 Wood, "Nonauthorial *Piers*," 494. See also, Scase, "Two *Piers Plowman* C-Text Interpolations."

15 Kane and Donaldson, eds., *Piers Plowman B*, 14–15, as cited by Wood, "Nonauthorial *Piers*," 483n3.

16 Magnani and Watt, "Queer Philology," 257–58. See, also, Sargent, "Organic and Cybernetic Metaphors," 212.

17 Freeman, "Erotohistory," 58.

18 Freeman, "Erotohistory," 58.

tion in law), according to Judith Butler, are used to produce the "unity and transmissibility of the nation": by reinforcing the State's power to confer recognition on to its citizens; by arbitrating over who deserves recognition; and by tying the possibility of recognition to key moments in the normative white cisheterosexual life course with a focus on the reproduction of white cisheterosexual subjects.[19] That is, the interests of stemmatic representation replicate the interests that prompted the founding of the field as I described them in Chapter 1. Stemmatics is invested in the chronopolitics of anachronism, which sees the medieval past/authorial original as both aspirational—as pure and unadulterated in its white cishetero masculinity—and as a black mirror for modernity, revealing its development and sophistication.[20] The visual rhetoric of the stemma, then, situates the manuscript within imperialist teleologies of modern cultural production, while also establishing the limits of what it might be allowed to signal (by viewing it as degradation of some superior originary text.)

Moreover, regardless of what its root represents (urtext, best text, or something else), the stemma proposes a linear reproductive hierarchy that transposes manuscript copying onto cishetero familial models. To understand how such models posit arboreal-genealogy as a means of organizing and controlling society, we might look no further than their medieval predecessors. Late medieval English and French genealogical rolls display the dynastic lineage of kings, connecting them, through roundels and branches, to their royal predecessors (see Figure 5). Genealogical rolls were produced in England from the end of the thirteenth-century until well into the sixteenth, with a peak during the reigns of Edward I and II (1272–1327), from which time at least forty rolls survive (not all of which are illustrated).[21] The early rolls are textually very similar—some are direct copies from known exemplars.[22] I take a richly produced example, British Library, MS Royal 14.E.vi, in order to emphasize the visual rhetorics at play in these works. The illustrated rolls typically begin with the early English heptarchy and end with a roundel containing an image of the reigning monarch: in this case, the last illuminated roundel is that of Edward I (r. 1272–1307) (see Figure 5,

19 Butler, *Undoing Gender*, 110–12, quote at 110.

20 See, also, Drimmer, "Queer Transmissions," esp. 7–8, with reference to Menon, *Unhistorical Shakespeare*, on the technological positivism and "heterotemporality" (7) built into this narrative.

21 de Laborderie, "First Manuals," 4.

22 See, for example Wakelin, *Designing English*, 70–71.

right). The historical commentary, an Anglo-French translation of an earlier Latin work, is organized around the diagram, subordinating text to image. "The English Royal dynasty," this framing suggests, "acts as the guiding principle of national history and is thus conferred a role in structuring its unfolding."[23]

According to Olivier de Laborderie's analysis, three significant features underpin the visual rhetoric of the roll: the imagery, the layout, and the format. The image of Edward I at the end of Royal 14.B.vi depicts him in a red and green frame, with a gold backdrop. Edward sits on a throne, wearing a blue robe, a red mantel, and a crown, and holding a sword and sceptre. He has these features in common with most of the other kings on the roll. Only a few are provided with further iconographic identifiers, like Edward the Confessor (r. 1042–1066), who holds his crown aloft to God in a gesture that presumably represents both his pious rejection of earthly wealth and his loss of the crown to the

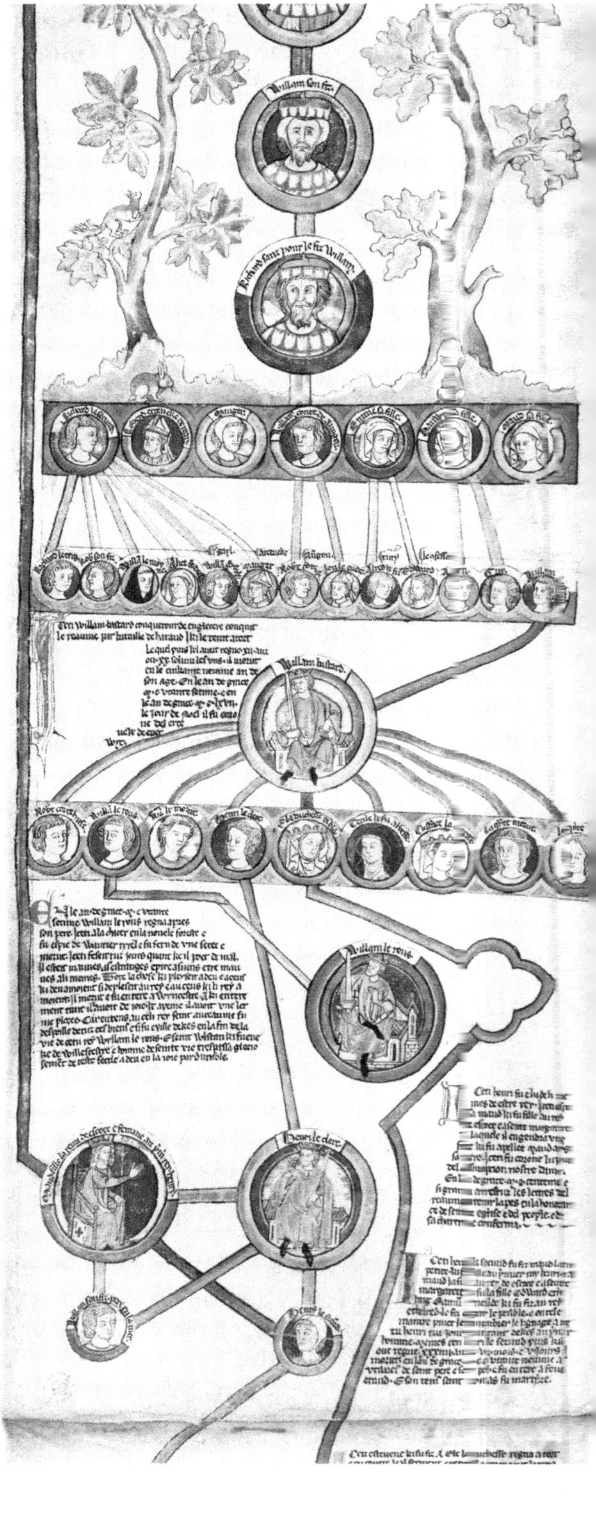

23 de Laborderie, "First Manuals," 10.

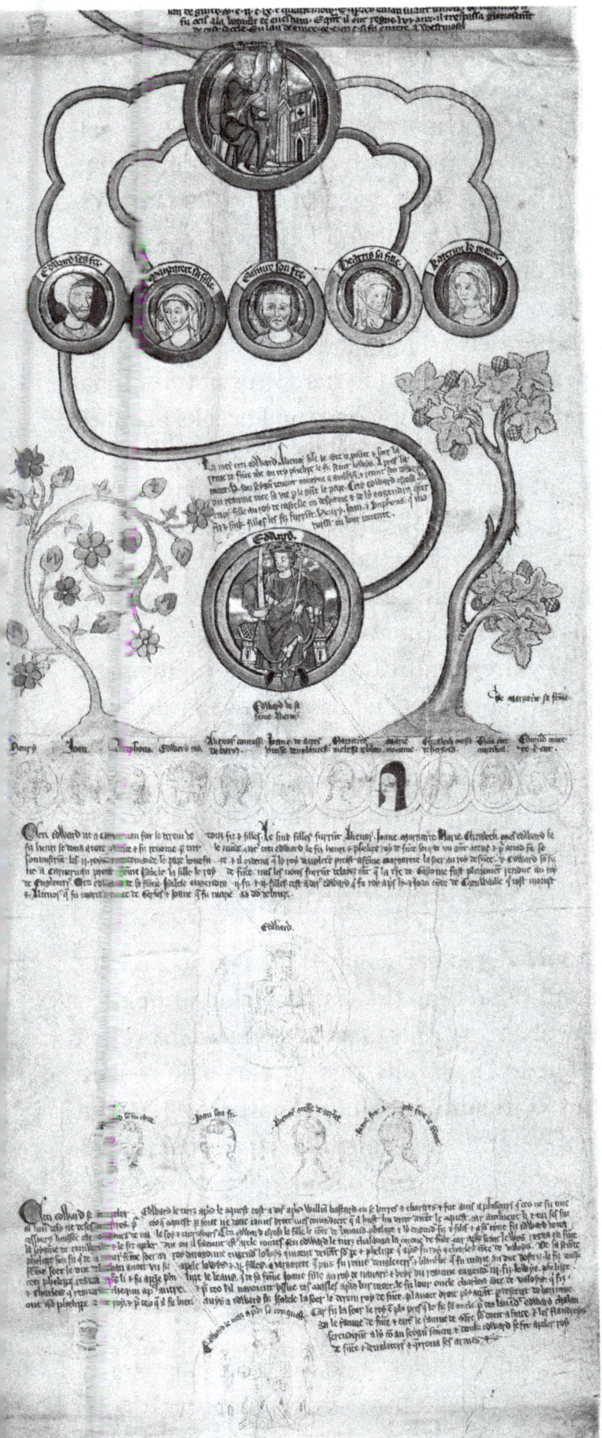

Figure 5. *Genealogical Chronicle of the English Kings*, ca. 1340. London, British Library, MS Royal 14.B.vi, m. 5 and 7. Reproduced by permission of the British Library.

Norman monarchs. Colour and position, de Laborderie has shown, can signal reputation and moral standing. However, overall, the artist aims for a "standardized aspect" (compare Figure 5, left).[24] De Laborderie draws a compelling comparison to Edward I's Great Seal, which also depicts an impersonal image of the monarch crowned and enthroned, facing forward, with sceptre and orb.[25] This is the imagery of authority and authentication, and the focus here is not on the individual, but on the institution. Despite the disruption of the Norman Conquest, and before it the Viking invasion of 1016, English kingship is depicted as uniform and unified.

The format and layout of the roll assert and historicize the continuity of the royal dynasty. The red and

---

24 de Laborderie, "First Manuals," 18.

25 de Laborderie, "First Manuals," 18.

blue connecting lines give the appearance of an unbroken chain descending from Ecgberht of Wessex (r. 802–839), offering legitimacy through continuous connection even if that connection occasionally had to be fudged. As if to underscore the point, trees "flank[...] two essential parts of the genealogy"—the lineage of the Norman dukes and the final roundel portraying Edward I—echoing upward facing Tree of Jesse diagrams, and, de Laborderie suggests, "a metaphor of fertility and fruitfulness."[26] However, as noted above, at certain points the chain does break. To remedy this, the artist of Royal 14.B.vi aligns the Kings along an imagined vertical line through the centre of the roll. In doing so, de Laborderie suggests, they raise the "genealogy of office" (*Amtsgenealogie*, per Ursula Nilgen) to the status of traditional familial relationships, "compensating [for] the unconcealed breaks of continuity as regards the hereditary devolution of the English crown."[27]

The visual rhetoric of the layout relies on selection: for kingship to take precedence, the field cannot become over-populated. Decisions over who to include and who to exclude reveal the political motivations at stake. For example, women are rarely highlighted (although daughters are sometimes included among the smaller horizontally arranged lines depicting a monarch's children), except where they are significant to sustaining dynastic claims. Such is the case for Mathilda of Scotland, who by dint of a thick vertical line connecting her to her mother St. Margaret of Scotland, daughter of Edward the Exile, and "an unusual graphic device" connecting her to her husband Henry I (r. 1100–1135) unites the Norman kings with their early English predecessors, sustaining a linear dynastic hegemony despite the visual upheaval caused by the Norman Conquest and the interleaving of the Norman dukes (Figure 5, left).[28]

The form of the roll both supported and participated in historicizing the authority of the English crown and regulating the transmission of English culture. "English records, from the Chancery rolls to most manor court rolls," writes de Laborderie, "were written down on rolls, this format could convey an impression of authority, if not of indubitable official nature. Whatever was kept on rolls must have been regarded by a good many people in late thirteenth-century England as coming from circles partaking, at some level, in the exercise of power." That is, as with the Plea and Memoranda Rolls of the

26 de Laborderie, "First Manuals," 14.

27 de Laborderie, "First Manuals," 17, citing Nilgen, "Amtsgenealogie und Amtsheiligkeit."

28 de Laborderie, "First Manuals," 12.

mayoral court discussed in the previous chapter, the format itself conveyed the authority of the crown to its audience. But it also afforded further claims to continuity and an unbroken historic precedent. The ability to "indefinitely extend" the document (through the addition of extra membrane), and to move backward and forward along it, places English kingship within a linear history with no "fix[ed]…temporal limit."[29] In fact, the incomplete plummet figures at the end of Royal 14.B.vi may indicate that at some point it was extended and updated by the scribe to include the reigns of Edward II (r. 1307–1327) and III (r. 1327–1377) (see Figure 5, right). Later rolls, like the fifteenth-century Middle English roll at the Beinecke Library, extend the history backward in time also, preceding the English heptarchy with biblical history and events from the Matter of Britain.[30] In this case, the roll traces the descent of the English crown from Adam and Eve in the Garden of Eden, suggesting that Edward IV's (r. 1461–1470, 1471–1483) authority was not just dynastic but divine, and charting a deterministic Christocentric English history that could easily be absorbed into modern white Christo-nationalist medievalisms. The makers (and—more pertinently—the royal and aristocratic owners and patrons) of these rolls argue, through their material and visual rhetorics, that royal authority and political power, and by extension cultural Englishness, was derived through unbroken patriarchal connection to an early heroic past and its Biblical precursors.

The epigraph for this section comes from the work of cultural theorist Sara Ahmed. She defines "compulsory heterosexuality" as the "accumulative effect of the repetition of the narrative of heterosexuality." Compulsory heterosexuality, Ahmed tells us, "shapes what it is possible for bodies to do, even if it does not contain what it is possible to be. Bodies take the shape of norms that are repeated over time and with force."[31] Ahmed's formulation originates from Adrienne Rich, who identifies the mechanics through which compulsory heterosexuality produces women as compliant heterosexual subjects, and in doing so reduces them to such subjects. By offering no other social formation as a viable option, "it leads the daughter to 'accept' incest/rape by her father, the mother to deny that it is happening, the battered wife to stay on with an abusive husband."[32] The cisheteropatriarchal logic of the stemma, in this case, shapes what is possible to ask about and do with manuscripts.

---

29 de Laborderie, "First Manuals," 8.

30 New Haven, Yale University, Beinecke Library, MS Marston 242.

31 Ahmed, *Cultural Politics of Emotion*, 145.

32 Rich, "Compulsory Heterosexuality," 645.

For Butler, compulsory heterosexuality is framed in terms of the control and replication of "culture" via the figure of "the poor child," who queer kinship structures threaten to sever from the normative nuclear family. They observe, in relation to debates surrounding the provision of marriage-type contracts between non-straight couples in the mid-2000s, that homophobic defences centring the rights of the child demonstrated anxieties—like those the genealogical rolls seek to arrest—surrounding "the transfer and reproduction of culture, where 'culture' carries with it implicit norms of racial purity and domination."[33] Here, cultural reproduction is equated with the production of (white cis straight) children, who will go on to produce their own children, within cisheteronormative family units where culture can be shared. "Children," Jules Gill-Peterson wrote in 2018, "by design deprived of civil rights and infantilized, are easy targets of political violence—just as easily, it turns out, as concerned adults can claim them for protection."[34] Today we find that the first wave of anti-trans legislation, which tends to focus on children—trans children's access to medical and social interventions and their ability to play sports—does so in the name of protecting cis and trans kids alike: protecting trans children from medicalization by overly "liberal" parents, or from making decisions they cannot take back. Legislation also tends to aim at protecting cis children from their trans counterparts, now cast as a capable and malicious threat. In both cases, "the poor child" must be simultaneously arrested and liberated for cishetero culture to progress as normal.

The investment of the cisheterosexist political establishment in the control and replication of "culture" is more overt, when the object at stake is not the format of the family, but cultural objects themselves. Here, the transmission of objects of (white western) culture—medieval manuscripts—becomes legible only through subscription to the dominant model for familial reproduction. Culture exists, stemmatic visual representations inform us, because the cisheteropatriarchal family model and the religio-political structures that produce it, makes it so. Queer and trans objects might be incorporated into such structures, through the application of the visual rhetoric of the stemma, or—as is Butler's concern—the legalization of "gay marriage." However, to do so implicates queer desire in cultural reproduction by restricting what queer can be: in legislation, Butler states, "desire and sexuality are ratified, justified, known, publicly instated, imagined as permanent, durable,"

33 Butler, *Undoing Gender*, 110.

34 Gill-Peterson, *Transgender Child*, 2.

but they are also limited to certain recognizable formations.[35] The incorporation of certain queer relationship structures—those that look most *like* their heterosexual counterparts—into state sanctioned and legislated life courses places other queer and trans modes of being outside of those structures. The result is a renewed focus on policing how relationships can fit the model, and to whom conferred protected status does or does not apply. To extend my comparison, whether or not a stemma is invested in the patriarchal model of the authorial original, whether or not the textual criteria by which variation is recognized have been adjusted, the visual rhetoric of the stemma affixes meaning to manuscripts, delimiting them in space and time.

Proponents of a revised "New Stemmatics" propose an approach that is agnostic to the source of variation (i.e., it removes the moralizing implications of assigning "error" to a scribe). Divergence from the hypothetical original is, from this perspective, no longer framed as a defect and all kinds of variations are admitted as evidence of textual relationships. New Stemmatic practitioners aim to produce computer-aided quantitative analysis of textual variation using all of the available variant data.[36] That analysis might be delimited and specified by admitting only "substantive variation," so that only variants that introduce significant modifications to the text are included in the model.[37]

Phylogenetics and cladistics present two overlapping computerized approaches. Genetic models of descent may appear to provide a natural analogue for manuscript transmission. Both describe a type of reproduction based on copying, in which encoded material (chromosomes/text) is selected and replicated along with any variation it may contain. But a book is not a genome. The scope of code at play in our DNA is at once much vaster than most books (three billion base pairs of DNA on one copy of the human genome compared to roughly three hundred fifty thousand characters in the book you are currently reading) and much more limited (most human chromosomes come in pairs of which one is copied from each parent, with twenty three pairs on a genome). Genetic variation is produced through mutation and recombination at certain points in the genome via predictable and discoverable biochemical processes. Although anomalies exist, large amounts of genetic material are "highly conserved" and not susceptible to variation (hence the oft repeated factoid that humans share roughly half

35 Butler, *Undoing Gender*, 111.

36 See Bordalejo, "New Stemmatics."

37 Bordalejo, "Genealogy of Texts," 566.

of their genetic code with a banana). Textual variation in manuscripts, on the other hand, comes out of a host of human factors both intentional and accidental, both easily explained and highly erratic, both textual and non-textual. Between any two humans, the level of genetic variation is roughly 0.1 percent, whereas, in a manuscript *directly* copied from an extant exemplar, Wakelin demonstrates divergence at a rate of about 3 percent.[38] Some scribes, of course, were more accurate copyists and others much, much less so.[39] As William Robins has argued, "genetic mutation, statistically considered, should happen at a similar rate over long periods of time" according to the molecular clock, "mak[ing] it possible to assign rough figures for the time that has elapsed on every branch of a genealogical tree, and... to compare different possible trees on the basis of how likely they are to have occurred given a standard rate of change." Manuscript copying, on the other hand, in unpredictable: a scribe may copy a manuscript immediately or select an exemplar hundreds of years after it was written.[40] Moreover, as Barabara Bordalejo explains, phylogenetic variation, which differentiates the evolutionary relationships between organisms, proceeds by binary logic. Genetic code is either changed to produce a differentiated organism or it is not. As a result, phylogenetic stemma are always bifid: one node cannot simultaneously split into multiple branches. However, there are plenty of cases in which one manuscript might be used to produce several copies, or one copy—like HM 114—made from several exempla.[41]

Cladistics (the unrooted diagrammatic representation of evolutionary changes prior to establishing lines of descent), as Robins shows, brings with it different issues. Peter Robinson has showed that a cladistic approach (provided by Robert O'Hara) produced a very similar stemma to the Old Icelandic poem *Svipdasmál* as his traditional approach.[42] However, his cladistic analysis of the *Wife of Bath's Prologue* drew considerable criticism, not least because in order to produce a workable unrooted tree, his team had to exclude fourteen manuscripts (using their own subjective criteria). Similarly, "rooting the tree and determining which state of the text was the earliest relied on traditional notions of error and authorship, not on any

38 National Institutes of Health, "Understanding Human Genetic Variation"; Wakelin, *Scribal Correction*, 46–47.

39 Robins, "Editing and Evolution," 113.

40 Robins, "Editing and Evolution," 113.

41 Bordalejo, "Genealogy of Texts," 566.

42 Robinson and O'Hara. "Cladistic Analysis."

new scientific or objective criterion provided by cladistics."[43] Moreover, the objectives of cladistic analysis, in which "sophisticated quantitative analyses borrowed from biology" are directed towards fine-tuning the comparison of variants in search of the authorial text, Robins suggest, are out of step with the trajectory of the field. "Being reliable in a statistical sense," he writes, "does not necessarily translate into a stemma being compelling in an interpretive sense." "In this and in other ways...cladistic analysis [does] not seem to have been set sufficiently within the larger context of what we surmise about...textual transmission."[44]

If we agree that stemmatic models misrepresent the practices of premodern authors, scribes, and readers, the ways those subject positions are prioritized, and the dynamics of movement between them, then another model that—with the aid of a computer—can reproduce those results in greater detail will only replicate its flaws. Recognizing a range of sources of variation is no help if, even as scholars acknowledge that textual variation comes in multiple forms that might enter the tradition in different ways and at different points, they continue to treat them homogenously in their analysis. New Stemmatics continues to treat variation as an abstract property of the text, which is both governed by and governs textual relations, and not as a material exigency that is situationally embedded. Indeed, Bordalejo clarifies that phylogenetic models present "textual data" not "literal representations" of historical realities. They are, she proposes, "an educated hypothesis created following a specific model" that imposes its own (in this case phylogenetic) assumptions.[45] Textual data is not un-situated or ahistorical and presenting it as such suggests that the manuscripts that contain it are static objects, frozen in time (or taken out of time) at the point that the manuscript was written.

This is not the material reality that governs the text: a copy of Chaucer's *Canterbury Tales* provides an apt example. The book was made for Jean d'Angoulême, younger brother of poet and duke, Charles d'Orléans, and grandson of Charles V of France. Angoulême's coat of arms—three *fleur-de lys* differenced by a lambel with three pennants, the first charged with a crescent—inhabits the opening initial (Figure 6).[46] Jean was a prisoner of the English crown for over three decades from 1412 to 1445, after he was given as a hostage to assure the Treaty of Buzançais when he was just thirteen.

43 Robins, "Editing and Evolution," 109.

44 Robins, "Editing and Evolution," 111 and 110.

45 Bordalejo, "Genealogy of Texts," 567.

46 Paris, Bibliothèque nationale de France, MS anglais 39 (*Canterbury Tales*), fol. 1r.

Figure 6. The first opening of the *Canterbury Tales*, 1412–1445. Paris, Bibliothèque nationale de France, MS anglais 39, fol. 1r. Courtesy of the Bibliothèque nationale de France. Source https://gallica.bnf.fr Bibliothèque nationale de France.

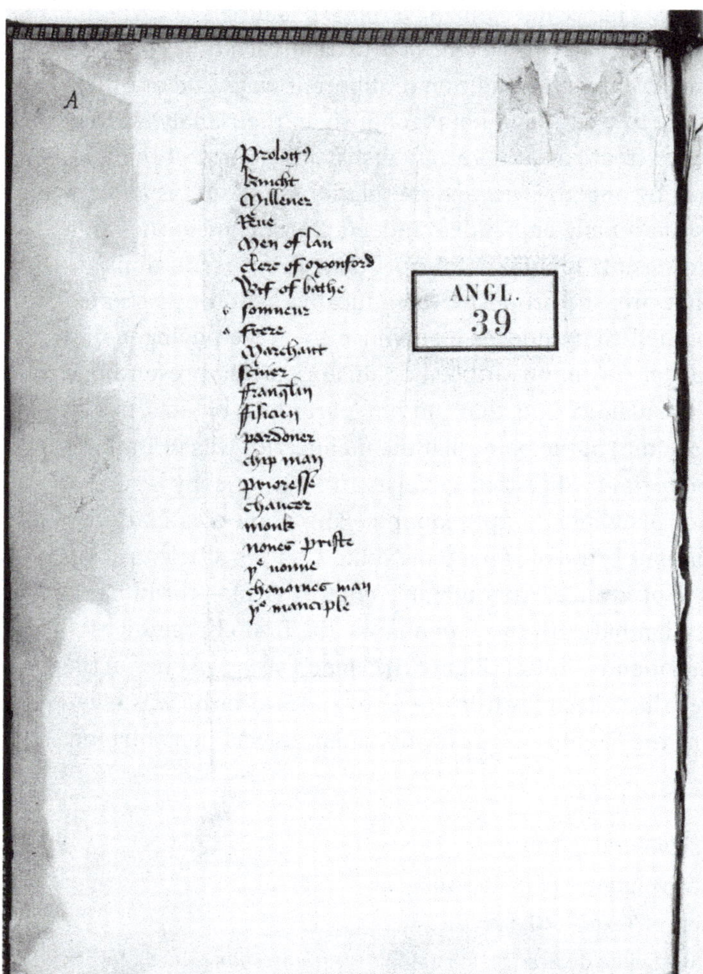

Figure 7. Jean d'Angoulême's contents page for his *Canterbury Tales*, copied in his own hand, 1412–1445. Paris, Bibliothèque nationale de France, MS anglais 39, fol. A. Courtesy of the Bibliothèque nationale de France. Source https://gallica.bnf.fr Bibliothèque nationale de France.

While in England, he collected, commissioned, and copied books, this manuscript among them. The scribe, who signs himself "Duxwurth Scriptor," wrote his English in a northern or north midlands dialect.[47] The exemplar Duxworth used seems to have been flawed, prompting him to make corrections from at least one other copy. Jean also made a series of corrections with reference to another copy of the *Tales*, perhaps different again.[48] A number of unique compositions—either by Duxworth or Jean but written in Duxworth's hand—supplement the corrections to fill larger gaps in the verse, while Latin intertexts abbreviate tales considered too vulgar, absurd, or sad.[49] These changes to the copy text rest on the back of a network of further material and textual connections: both in the form of the manuscripts they consulted to correct their readings and in the more diffuse web of literary influences that shaped their written responses to the text. At what stage, we might ask, was this text considered finished? When and where should its progress be crystalized within the static structure of the stemma?

The manuscript's geographic and temporal status is further complicated by the use that Jean made of it. His *Tales* manuscript was probably made by the English scribe while Jean was captive in England. However, on his release he took many of his books back to France, and at the time of his death in 1467 the manuscript was listed among the contents of his library in Cognac.[50] The coloured capitals appear to be the work of a French artist, perhaps supplied after Jean's return to the Continent.[51] Jean also added a table of contents, which is now stuck to the front pastedown (Figure 7).[52] The contents list is brief giving only the occupation of the pilgrim responsible for each tale. But, despite its brevity, it is—like Duxworth's additions—linguistically mixed. It begins with the Latin "Prologus (prologue)," followed by the English "Knicht (knight)," "Millener (milliner)," and "Reue (reeve)." Further down the list are found the French, or French-rooted, "somneur (summoner)," "frere (friar)," and "Marchant (merchant)," while the penultimate entry, "chanoins man (canon's man)," employs a French-English hybrid.[53] How do we account for

---

47 BnF, MS anglais 39, fol. 83v; Crow, "*The Reeves Tale*"; Crane, "Duxworth Redux," 17.

48 Crow, "John of Angoulême," 96.

49 Crane, "Duxworth Redux," 18.

50 The inventory is found in Paris, Archives nationales de France, P 1403, nos. 38–39. The *Canterbury Tales* manuscript is item number 37.

51 Crane, "Duxworth Redux," 24.

52 BnF, MS anglais 39, fol. A.

53 I thank J. R. Mattison for this observation, which she has discussed in conference papers, and which prompted me to attend to this manuscript.

these mixed-language additions by a Continental French writer, influenced by a series of other works with their own communal networks, and in a manuscript that has spent most of its life in Continental libraries, in a static system that asks for markers of sustained but atomized linear chronological progress.

My objections here should not suggest that a conception of the form of the text (or even some abstract hypothetical originary text) is not important. But it is only a part, and I would argue a rather small one, of the story of what texts can do and their existence across and through time. Efforts to displace the morally freighted category of error in favour of more contextually situated understandings of variation—coincident variation, copying mistakes, addition, alteration, correction, and self-conscious editing—or to supplant the search for authorship with more neutral constructions—of the archetype or the best text—do not address the visual rhetoric of the stemmatic diagram.

Sargent explains the deterministic ascription of meaning in different genetic terms: "an arboriform stemma falsely imputes to the developmental scheme a genetic logic comparable to that by which an acorn can only grow into an oak tree."[54] The significance of a manuscript, in other words, is pre-determined by its location on a stemma, which is paradoxically used to decide whether its variants should bear textual weight. The increasing popularity of low-cost mail in genetic ancestry testing services (GATS), V. Jo Hsu argues, has resurfaced the white supremacist underpinnings of deterministic genetic logics. These services often appeal to an essentializing model that promises that "DNA encodes indelible truths about who you are and 'what makes you unique.'" In actuality, the tests compare key markers on a subject's DNA with global population data collected by the Human Genome Project, in order to present a break down of "ancestry" or "human variation" via "continental taxonomies (Native American, European, Asian, Oceania, and Africa)" that substitute as "an approximation of race." "Though GATS (claim to have) emerged from opposing scientific motives" (celebrating "what makes you unique"), Hsu notes, "scientific racism established the primary categories through which we narrativize new data."[55] Indeed, the underlying racializing logic of such tests has made them particularly popular with white nationalists looking for evidence of their racial purity.[56] Importantly, the way

54 Sargent, "Organic and Cybernetic Metaphors," 204.

55 Hsu, *Constellating Home*, 112.

56 See Panofsky and Donovan, "Genetic Ancestry Testing."

GATS are positioned as indicative of individual identity ("what makes you unique"), "papers over" racialized histories of "conquest and exploitation," privilege and subordination, "with biological determinism."[57] Similarly, the position of a manuscript within an arboreal-stemma act as a measure of its significance, papering over the individual features that make it interesting. This is not only misrepresentation, but limitation.

What is needed, Hsu concludes, are ways to "conceive of familial lineages ..that disrupt, challenge, and reinvent the categories that have isolated and harmed queer diasporic subjects."[58] For manuscript studies, we need ways to understand the relations between manuscript, text, and material text that disrupt their use in white supremacist and cisheteropatriarchal cultural production and recognize their status as contingent, socially embedded, and relational cultural products.

Queer Families, Trans Lives

The visual-rhetorical impasse of the stemma, New Stemmatics tells us, is a problem of presentation. The bipartite stemma, we are reminded, offers the shortest possible route between the extant witnesses and a hypothetical original. It is not a "literal representation" of the relationships between manuscripts, but a measure of agreement or disagreement within a textual group.[59] Thus, Ben Salemans uses the computational genetics program *PAUP** (Phylogenetic Analysis Using Parsimony *and other methods) to model a series of unrooted stemma for the *Lai de l'ombre*—which a century earlier caused Joseph Bédier to doubt the usefulness of the genealogical method—demonstrating that each of the eleven possible arrangements that Bédier proposed for the lai's stemma encode the same textual relationships. The "chain," Salemans shows, remains the same, just the placement of its "root" has changed.[60] In response, Salemans advocates an approach that, rather than determining the root of the stemma *a priori*, orients (or opts not to orient) the chain after variation has been assessed. For Salemans and other New Stemmaticists, this observation overcomes any qualms that scholars might have about the stemma's apparent hierarchical investments. But as book historians we know that the presentation of information is not

57 Hsu, *Constellating Home*, 112.

58 Hsu, *Constellating Home*, 113.

59 See Bordalejo above, for example.

60 Salemans, "Building Stemmas," 34–35.

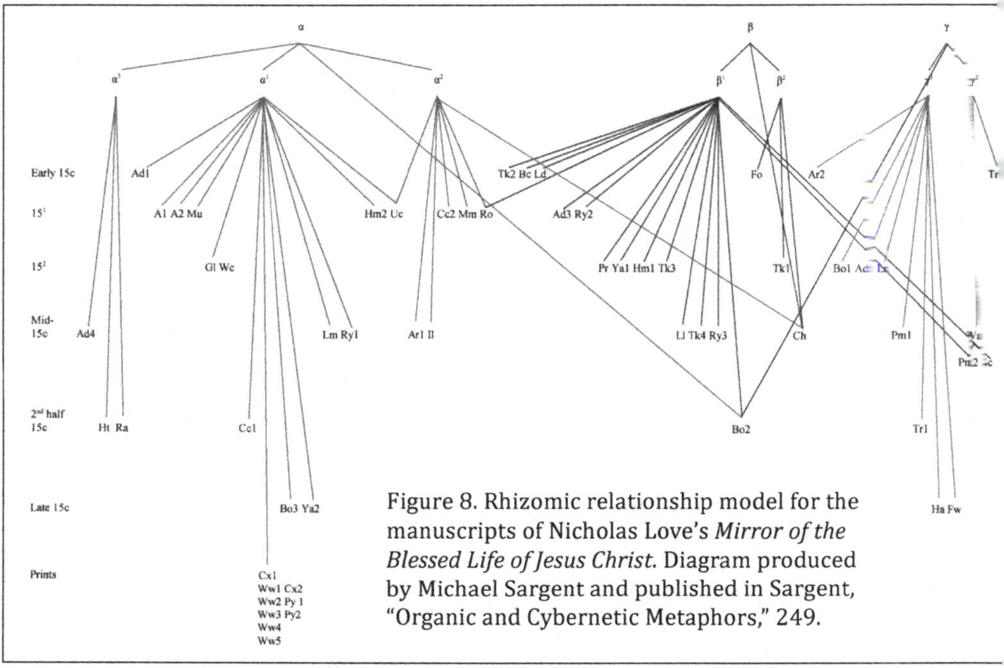

Figure 8. Rhizomic relationship model for the manuscripts of Nicholas Love's *Mirror of the Blessed Life of Jesus Christ*. Diagram produced by Michael Sargent and published in Sargent, "Organic and Cybernetic Metaphors," 249.

neutral. I have shown above that, whether rooted before or after complete variant analysis, arboriform stemma are oriented towards particular intellectual outcomes (constructing canonicity, introducing hierarchies, and fixing textual objects within a progressivist temporal frame) and implicate manuscripts in the construction of oppressive socio-political realities (those which benefit from a teleological and positivist formulation of white Euro-American society.)

Unrooted forms remove some visual hierarchies but retain other stemmatic problems, as Sargent explains. They do not solve, for example, the inability of recensionist stemmatics to differentiate between sources of textually similar variation. Nor can they tell us more about the relationships between manuscripts (only their textual differences) or allow for connections between nodes.[61]

Sargent's solution is the rhizome. Prior to Sargent, David Greetham and Michael Stoltz also found the rhizome a "useful" model.[62] Inspired by Deleuze and Guattari's *A Thousand Plateaus*, each employs the rhizome as a means of avoiding the patrilineal assumptions of the arboriform stemma

61 Sargent, "Organic and Cybernetic Metaphors," 241.

62 Sargent, "Organic and Cybernetic Metaphors," 247.

and envisioning the practice of textual criticism beyond recension.[63] "The rhizome," Sargent imagines, "like a mushroom ring or a circular stand of larch trees, has multiple "points of origin" at the surface (every time a rhizomorphic radicle breaks the surface of the ground, it sends up another tree), branching and interconnecting in ways whose "direction" (mother plant to daughter plant) cannot be determined."[64] This concept of non-hierarchical interconnection allows Sargent to posit an edition of Nicholas Love's *Mirror of the Blessed Life of Jesus Christ* where every manuscript text can be viewed in relation to every other by varying the base text depending on where the reader enters the rhizome (Figure 8).[65] If we enact the rhizome not just as an apt visual metaphor for the (unrooted, anti-hierarchical) relationships between witnesses to a textual tradition, but as a model of connectivity and production, what else might we learn about medieval books and their transmission? I suggest that the rhizome, particularly as it is interpreted and developed in trans criticism, presents a conceptual alternative to the stemma that recognizes the situationally embedded enmeshment of textual production. The rhizome offers an understanding of manuscript production that is transferable, relational, that develops and changes across time, and that is always in process.

Deleuze and Guattari's conception of the rhizome also departs from a critique of "arborescent" logic. This structure, they note, "has dominated… Western thought, from botany to biology and anatomy, but also gnosiology, theology, ontology, all of philosophy."[66] Trees, they suggest, provide a model that can only account for bifurcating linear descent. Such models force dualist logic. Thus, for Deleuze and Guattari, "[a]rborescent systems are hierarchical systems with centers of significance and subjectification, central automata like organized memories. In the corresponding models, an element only receives information from a higher unit, and only receives a subjective affection along preestablished paths."[67] The nodes in an arborescent system, can always be traced back through bifid connections to the root, and share no connections to the nodes at the same remove from the root, but on different branches. The result is a unidirectional top-down hierarchy, in

63 Greetham, "Phylum–Tree–Rhizome"; Stoltz, "Linking the Variance."

64 Sargent, "Organic and Cybernetic Metaphors," 247.

65 Sargent, "Organic and Cybernetic Metaphors," 247–51. See also, Sargent, "Hidden in Plain Sight," 72n12.

66 Deleuze and Guattari, *Thousand Plateaus*, 18.

67 Deleuze and Guattari, *Thousand Plateaus*, 16.

which the root represents both the pure and unadulterated original and the source of linear progress, and from which the outcome is overdetermined. Further, arborescent thinking operates by reproduction, its objective to replicate the structure that came before, and its logic is therefore totalizing (all nodes point back to the root). So far, so recensionist.

When Deleuze and Guattari introduce the rhizome, it is in relation to the production of books. In this case, it is their own book that they constitute as an "assemblage" that "functions" in relation to other things—other objects, including other books, but also dematerialized linguistic and social structures (or structures materialized otherwise)—that operate outside of and against pre-determinate hierarchies of power.[68] Crucially, unlike the arborescent stemma, which figures the text as a self-sufficient reproductive entity, the rhizome recognizes the entanglement of actors and forces that come together in the production of a book as materialized text. "There is no difference," proffer Deleuze and Guattari, "between what a book talks about and how it is made."[69]

The rhizome is defined by seven key principles:

Connection. The rhizome does not fix the order or direction of connection between objects; any node may be connected to any other. The relationship is not mono-directional. The connections are mobile and fluid, evolving, spreading, and changing.

Heterogeneity. The nodes in a rhizome need not be textual or linguistic, or even ontologically the same: "semiotic chains of every nature are connected to very diverse modes of coding (biological, political, economic, etc.) that bring into play not only different regimes of signs but also states of things of differing status."

Multiplicity. The object is not unitary. It is not a central "pivot" around which other objects, forces, and cultural signifiers circulate (and which can therefore be reproduced), but an enmeshment of all of those things. Hence, the term node used above to describe the placement of participant aspects is a misnomer. Deleuze and Guattari prefer to understand these aspects as "lines" or "planes," which, because they are flat, cannot be split according to binary logic, but proliferate and multiply through space.

68 Deleuze and Guattari, *Thousand Plateaus*, 4 and 7–8.

69 Deleuze and Guattari, *Thousand Plateaus*, 4.

Asignifying rupture. When the relationship between objects in an arborescent model is broken, it cannot be reformed. The branch is severed from the root. In a rhizome, breaking allows for remaking. Relationships are constantly forming and reforming. A line may take off in a single direction ("a line of flight"), but it will also retain connections, and form new connections, within the whole system.

Cartography. The rhizome is not an image produced through replication or genetic reproduction ("tracing"). It is a process, a "map" that "is open and connectable in all of its dimensions; it is detachable, reversible, susceptible to constant modification." The rhizome is mobile and accessible from different perspectives.

Decalcomania. The rhizome cannot be described in totality: to do so is to convert it to a fixed structure (to trace it) and thereby shut down its possibilities. However, objects can always be resituated within the rhizome. "A new rhizome may form in the heart of a tree, the hollow of a root, the crook of a branch."[70]

For trans and queer studies, the rhizome offers an alternative to the patrilineal reproductive logics that govern the arborescent family tree. Deleuze and Guattari describe the rhizome as "an antigenealogy," that "operates by variation, expansion, conquest, capture, offshoots"; "a liberation of sexuality not only from reproduction but also from genitality."[71] Alternative modes of family building—families that take shape outside of patrilineal reproductive frameworks—have been crucial to many queers, for whom (cishetero) familial ties are often fraught. The rhizome offers a model for relationships that emerge from a breakdown in the natal family unit (4), that prioritize multiple, variable connections (1 and 3), and that allow for discrepancy between the subject(s) and object(s) of affections, their modes of expression, and the overlapping forms of closeness these relationships entail (2).

Such relationships may be temporally or spatially multidirectional. On reflecting on her friendships with queer colleagues, Sedgwick notes that they "deroutinized the temporality" that characterizes heterosexual "generational relations."[72] Jack Halberstam defines queer temporality as the model "that emerge[s]...once one leaves the temporal frames of bourgeois

70 See Deleuze and Guattari, *Thousand Plateaus*, 7–16.

71 Deleuze and Guattari, *Thousand Plateaus*, 10 and 18.

72 Sedgwick, "Paranoid Reading," 25–26.

reproduction and family, longevity, risk/safety, and inheritance" behind.[73] Trans people especially may experience time as a series of compressions, extensions, and abruptions: the typical markers of the overdetermined straight cis life course—infancy, adolescence, marriage (and divorce), retirement etc.—may be inaccessible, delayed, repeated, or skipped.[74] For Julian Carter, "transitional time" moves "forward, backward, sideways, [and] tangential[ly]."[75] Carter's essay, which is in part a commentary on the trans historicizing practices of dancer and choreographer Sean Dorsey, presents a "vision of transitional time and transitioning bodies, as dynamic and relational negotiations of wrongness... Anticipation, retroflexion, and continuity co-exist in the same body, at the same moving moment of space and time."[76] As Ruth Pearce summarizes, transitional time is "the embodied coexistence of past, present and future, along with physical and social changes that might occur, will occur, have occurred. I read this as futurity without linearity...we can regard the transitioning body as simultaneously rooted in a future through anticipation—or even multiple, differently gendered futures—and in the past through social readings that sex the body's physical frame."[77] The rhizome defies expectations that one's life, and the relationships formed across it, should be either temporally linear (descendent) or biologically guaranteed. Instead, it presents the possibility of relationships that are communally embedded, unconstrained, and fluctuating in connection across a lifetime.

By introducing temporal and relational mobility into manuscript affiliations, we can imagine connections between multiple textual branches of a tradition. Such connections might change across a period of writing, reading, or ownership. For instance, there is no longer pressure to place the harmonized copy of *Piers Plowman* in HM 114 within one familial group. Instead, we can understand this copy of the text as connected to multiple groups, with priority given to particular connections at particular points. But, more importantly, the rhizome positions the manuscript in relation to objects and forces beyond the textual. Understanding the rhizome as a network of interconnected forces and actions working on people and objects, allows us to

73 Halberstam, *Queer Time and Place*, 6.

74 José Esteban Muñoz terms these normative experiences "straight time": Muñoz, *Cruising Utopia*, 7.

75 Carter, "Dancing in the Folds of Time," 130.

76 Carter, "Dancing in the Folds of Time," 131.

77 Pearce, *Understanding Trans Health*, 124.

consider each moment of manuscript production and transmission as situationally embedded. In the case of the harmonized *Piers*, that might start with the acknowledgement that, as Scase observes, the same sections of the C-text prologue were interpolated at a different point in another *Piers Plowman* manuscript, and that both manuscripts were copied by scribes associated with the London Guildhall.[78] A manuscript rhizome centred on these manuscripts, then, might build a picture of the Guildhall copyists negotiating between different versions of the text and their own perceptions of authority. Such models exchange the abstracted text in favour of one that is materially situated. In doing so, they make explicit the socio-political structures—of the Guildhall, the patron, and the exemplar—that govern cultural production (rather than visually participating in those structures).

"A rhizome has no beginning or end; it is always in the middle, between things, interbeing, *intermezzo*."[79] Very rarely, in models of textual transmission, can we evidence the root of the chain. Perhaps, on the rare occasion that an autograph manuscript survives, we might find ourselves somewhere near the beginning; but even then, a composition does not spring on to the parchment fully formed. Medieval authors compiled, collated, drafted, translated, so that every composition represents a network (rhizome) of dimensions, influences, and activities. Contrary to the chronopolitics of recensionist manuscript studies, which prefers to look for beginnings and ends, manuscripts operate from the middle. Embracing the in-between means first dispensing with the idea of the manuscript as product—a complete endpoint from which we can assert textual or cultural authority. As Elaine Treharne shows, manuscripts may exist at many stages of completion at different points in their life, each of which can be figured by those they exist in relation to as a kind of wholeness.[80] "Contrary to a deeply routed belief," Deleuze and Guattari assure us, "the book is not an image of the world."[81] It is not an unproblematic copy (tracing), nor a model of textual relations. Instead, the rhizome allows us to understand not just scribal copying, but the manuscript itself, as processual. It is enmeshed in the objects and forces—social, political, cultural—that brought it in to being and that continue to sustain

78 London, Senate House Library, MS S.L. V.88; Scase, "Two *Piers Plowman* C-Text Interpolations"; see Wood, "Nonauthorial *Piers*," for an updated findings and an account of the scholarly debate around these manuscripts.

79 Deleuze and Guattari, *Thousand Plateaus*, 25.

80 See Treharne, *Perceptions of Medieval Manuscripts*.

81 Deleuze and Guattari, *Thousand Plateaus*, 11.

it. Understanding a manuscript as process provides a better picture of the coming together of material and action that is not overdetermined, to echo Sargent's critique.

In the case of Jean d'Angoulême's *Canterbury Tales*, we encounter a manuscript that has been variously complete at different times in its making and use. The "defective"—but presumably wholly written—text was corrected with reference to at least one, possibly two other copies, with additional original compositions widening the manuscript rhizome from other manuscripts of the *Canterbury Tales* to a broader swathe of textual influences. A recensionist approach to the manuscript might discount those corrections and additions, or even the manuscript as a whole, but an approach that understands the manuscript as always in process could see this book as representative of a continuum of textual and material influence. The textual tradition as represented by this manuscript demonstrates the movement and availability of exemplars; the practices of a reader not concerned with authenticity but with a particular vision of the reading experience; and the bookish aspirations of Jean as a patron who reread and perfected his books. The contents list that Jean produced is one indication of a process of textual refinement that included removing content that he or his scribe found distasteful, as well as adding and correcting. Modern editions, and analysis like the present discussion, participate in these material relations, extending the temporal frame of the rhizome into the present. Prioritizing manuscripts that demonstrated these extended relational networks might displace patriarchal authority in favour of diffuse and variable use. It provides a gateway for understanding reading as participant in the transmission of texts, while recognizing that the perspective of the scribe and the reader—or the scribe-reader—was always partial, limited, interrupted. And because of that, could be creative and co-constitutive.

While manuscripts may be "in the middle," they are not at the centre. The rhizome is not static, it continues to move, break off, and reform. As queer and trans rhizomics remind us, the planar movement of the rhizome resists chronology and organization. This planar movement is part of scribal production also. Wakelin's analysis of the various habits of correction employed by scribes copying middle English texts shows that they developed patterns of interaction with their exemplars that might be lateral, cyclical, and/or fractured. Most scribes, most of the time, tried to transfer the text of the exemplar directly to their copy, however material circumstance might prompt other behaviours, including leaving gaps, cycling back to difficult areas, rereading, substitution, and emendation. Changes in movement (intellectual and physical) might be momentary or they may take place over long periods, even generations, as new exemplars were acquired and consulted. The relation between copyist and exemplar, then, is not one of mechanical reproduction, but a necessarily embodied experience requiring prolonged and multi-directional negotiation between environmental constraints, an abstract conception of the work, and the realities of the material text.[82]

Each scribe, just like every reader that follows them, presents a new way into the manuscript map—the manuscript and its variants are not a replicable experiment. As a result, any single vision of the manuscript-rhizome will be limited. Or as Greetham puts it, "we can never find a ground from which to perceive the structure at large (because it is incomprehensible, cannot be 'grasped')."[83] Consequently, the relationality of the queer rhizome must be communally constituted: the manuscript is required to act as a social space. Due to its vastness, a vision of the rhizomic-network may only be constructed through the communal vision implicated by the multiplicity of the rhizome itself. In fact, I suggest, interacting with the rhizome enters us into its network. Such is the implication of Jafari S. Allen's "Black/queer rhizomatics," which he describes as a "habit of mind" that is "processual—not teleological or 'narrativized in advance'" and that "progresses through interdisciplinary juxtaposition and communal relations."[84] Allen's students read through a rhizome of Black queer scholarship and artwork presented against generic or chronological divisions. In so doing, they enter into relation with the authors and creators they encounter and form their own communal bonds and commitments: "Today," Allen assures, "the runway on which Black/queer youth turn it—new-way intellectual death drops, duck walks, and poses—is not 'new' in the sense of without precedent or untraceable or cut off from its people. Theirs is another iteration emerging from legendary attitudes and grammars."[85] "[Q]ueers survive," Elizabeth Freeman suggests, "through the ability to invent or seize pleasurable relations between bodies…across time."[86] Medieval manuscripts, this book proposes, offer one venue through which a shared politic, based on intergenerational, transtemporal kinship relations, might be built.

---

82 Wakelin, *Scribal Correction*.

83 Greetham, "Phylum—Tree—Rhizome," 108.

84 Allen, "Black/Queer Rhizomatics," 34 and 28 respectively.

85 Allen, "Black/Queer Rhizomatics," 38.

86 Freeman, *Time Binds*, 58.

Constellating Manuscript Witnesses

As a system of thought, rhizomes offer manuscript studies a means of embedding our objects of investigation within wider, non-hierarchical, and crucially unrooted networks imbricated in a range of transtemporal social and material formations. Such frameworks recognize each manuscript copy as an independent object produced under specific social and textual conditions, by scribes with their own particular sets of concerns. The questions we can ask, therefore, become less about how a manuscript relates to the textual tradition, and more about how manuscripts of a textual tradition relate to one another, to the world around them, and crucially, to an ongoing community of users. How do we relate to these manuscripts? The rhizome resituates the manuscript from the static ahistorical and sanitized realm of the research library to the dynamic and continual arena of the book in use. However, marshalling the ever-expanding network of connections a rhizome might present—Greetham's "incomprehensible" structure—and making meaningful sense of those connections is—I have suggested—not necessarily possible or desirable.

Hsu develops their method of "constellating home"—used in their monograph to negotiate, through interconnected story-paths, the "multiple displacements" experienced by QTAPI (queer and trans Asian and Pacific Islanders)—out of decolonial knowledge-making processes.[87] In *As We Have Always Done*, Leanne Betasamosake Simpson describes the "constellation" as "an organizing concept" that positions Indigenous groups and individuals practicing various "everyday acts of resurgence" into a political formation capable of radical co-resistance.[88] Constellations are "strategic, relational arrangements" that are dynamic, hold their subjects in relation to one another, and accommodate multiple modes of being. Community constellations open up "lines of flight," expanding capacity, allowing for collaboration, cross-pollination, and improvisation, and providing means to navigate "pathways through a contemporary political landscape increasingly defined by blockages and impasses."[89] Constellations might be socio-political, but they can also be conceptual, material, or linguistic: Jarrett Martineau analyzes the practices of art and music collectives; Malea Powell and

87 Hsu, *Constellating Home*, 116.

88 Simpson, *As We Have Always Done*, 216 and 192 (and throughout).

89 Martineau, "Creative Combat," 50.

the Cultural Rhetorics Theory Lab offer a framework for Native story-work.[90] For these scholars and activists, constellation is both the method through which story is told and shared (through repetition and iteration that adjusts the hearers perspective at each encounter) and a measure of the community relations it represents (as intersectional, geographically dispersed and displaced and multigenerational). For Hsu, constellating stories through their structures, themes, and poetics provides a way of constructing the space of home among displaced communities.

Using constellation to describe manuscript relations involves hazards. Manuscripts are not neutral technologies. The medieval European manuscripts that survive, which form the primary focus of this book, transmit discourses of power, especially those of law and religion, that are bound up in the building and retention of empire (see Chapter 2). Manuscript studies is not a neutral, let alone minority, discourse—as discussed in Chapter 1, the field of manuscript studies takes its cues from eighteenth- and nineteenth-century imperial rhetorics active in the founding of the modern university. Constellations, on the other hand, are decolonial technologies. The constellation, as Simpson defines it, produces "flight paths out of settler colonialism" by connecting acts of "radical resurgence, generative refusal, and reciprocal recognition" into a collective political movement that circumvents colonial power structures.[91]

Crucially, constellations are not equally available to everyone: they "are coded mappings...for those with star literacy," the significance of which is "opaque" to colonizers not embedded in Nishnaabeg ways of knowing.[92] In part, it is its opacity that affords the constellation its navigational power. Opacity and uncertainty are tactics of resistance to identity politics, which Indigenous and decolonial knowledge keepers see deriving from a colonial politics of recognition that seeks to categorize, legislate, and assimilate or eradicate minority groups. Refusing identification is protection and resistance.[93] Populist media sources have associated queer and trans people with

---

90 Martineau; "Creative Combat"; and, for example, Riley-Mukavetz and Powell. "Making Native Space." As far as I can tell, the Cultural Rhetorics Theory Lab is no longer active. Members included Malea Powell, Daisy Levy, Andrea Riley-Mukavetz, Marilee Brooks-Gillies, Maria Novotny, and Jennifer Fisch-Ferguson: see "Our Story Begins Here." See, also, the artist collective, Black Constellation.

91 Simpson, *As We Have Always Done*, 213.

92 Simpson, *As We Have Always Done*, 212–13.

93 Simpson, *As We Have Always Done*, 175–80. See, in this context, Coulthard, *Red Skin White Masks*; Simpson, *Mohawk Interruptus*.

a shift towards identity politics. Conservative pundits cite the existence of trans people and their desire for legal rights, in particular, as evidence of the divisiveness of identity politics. First, it is important that we call such claims what they are—dog whistles from the right that politicize trans lives in an effort to sow suspicion and cast resentment on to marginalized communities.[94] Indeed, in light of such attacks, which so easily give way to state-sanctioned (and state-led) violence, we might reflect on the value of embracing obscurity. However, we should also engage thoughtfully with where the projects of claiming and obscuring identity categories intersect, especially if those projects operate from within settler colonial academic institutions. To that end, I reiterate two priorities for this book: first, I use trans (and queer) not as labels that define people according to any external markers, but as an expansive category of structural insistence; and second, I use trans critique as a means of dismantling legacies of white supremacism and cisheterosexism. When applied in the manuscript studies context, as anywhere else, constellating cannot be extractive. It should emerge from critique and seek to resurface, in whatever temporary formations those take, displaced and unseated ways of knowing that refuse oppressive institutional structures.

Constellations can temporarily stabilize and delimit rhizomic networks. Like rhizomes, constellations may present a mix of objects, people, and ideas. For Hsu, this mixture includes "linguistic, visual, and other cultural artifacts."[95] However, unlike in a rhizome, where possible connections are always changing and multiplying, a constellation requires selection. For a constellation to be meaningful it must include some stars and exclude others, picking a pattern out of the night sky. The selected stars present a narrative that collocates the shape of the constellation in the sky and the stories represented by that shape. However, when the stories are over, our vision or our concentration is broken, or the daylight comes around, the selected stars may recede, becoming ontologically indistinct from all other stars in the sky. Stars in a constellation work in concert with one another and with the negative space that surrounds them (allowing them to be picked out and joined together), while remaining part of a larger—ever-moving and growing—whole. The rhizome of the night sky, then, is temporarily delimited in the form of the constellation, but it is not fixed in that form. Consequently, I look to constellating as informant to the practice of describing,

---

94 For in depth analysis of such aims, see, for instance, Cannon, *Politicization of Trans Identity*.

95 Hsu, *Constellating Home*, 130.

understanding, and making decisions about rhizomic manuscript relations. Where the rhizome presents renewed possibility, emancipating the manuscript from heteropatriarchal organizational structures, the constellation directs that disruption toward alternative, resistive, redistributive social narratives.

Constellations situate networks of relations in space and time. As Simpson reminds us, our view of the stars and their relation to one another is intimately bound up with place. In the northern hemisphere, Ursa Major (part of which is known colloquially to anglophone American settlers as the Big Dipper, to British English-speakers as the Plough, and to the Nishnaabeg as the Gchi Ojiig (Great Fisher) formation and story)[96] is visible all year round, but from points between the equator and 25° latitude south the constellation is only visible close to the horizon, most prominently in the spring, while at points south of this the main asterism (the Plough part of the constellation) cannot be seen. In cities all but the largest and closest stars disappear in the glare of artificial streetlights. "[C]onstellations are place-based relationships," Simpson explains, "and land-based relationships are the foundation of Indigenous thought,"[97] whether that land be, like Simpson's, on the ground in Nogojiwanong (known by settlers as Peterborough, Ontario), the collective "Nishnaabewin (Nishnaabeg intelligence)," or like Hsu the more metaphysical claim to a space to call home.[98] In either case, place is restored by carving out space within dominant discourses (in neoliberal political norms grounded in capitalist imperialism, and limited prejudicial images of Asian American culture respectively) to effect resistance. One objective of this book is to build a home within the discipline of manuscript studies for trans, queer, and minoritized students and scholars. But it is also to demonstrate that transness already occupies manuscript spaces. Constellating manuscripts against rooted stemma—according to other non-genealogical relational bonds (as I will in Chapter 4)—and prioritizing (as a rhizome alone cannot and should not) the connections that resonate trans and queer experience, presents a tactic for uncovering such formations.

Constellations build relationships across time. When we look at the sky we are seeing back in time. The starlight that reaches our eyes may have travelled many hundreds of years to get to us (the light from our own sun is

96 See Simpson, *As We Have Always Done*, 214–15.

97 Simpson, *As We Have Always Done*, 213.

98 For Nishnaabewin, see Simpson, *As We Have Always Done*, 22–25, and Simpson, *Short History of the Blockade*.

already eight minutes old when it reaches Earth). Alioth, the brightest star in the Plough asterism, is around 300 million years old, and 82.5 lightyears away. Stars in the same constellation may be millions of miles away from one another, and millions of years apart in age. The Nishnaabeg, Simpson clarifies, do not "dissect time into past, present, and future."[99] So, when Simpson invokes ancestral relations, it is with the understanding that her ancestors' knowledge, life, and experiences play active roles in her actions in the present, and in the construction of "an elsewhere in the here; a present future beyond the imaginative and territorial bounds of colonialism."[100] Simpson's "present future"—the shared knowledge of futurity in the now—chimes with Ruth Pearce's concept of trans temporal anticipation, which redeploys the (often negative) experiences of the past as a strategy to orient oneself toward a different and better future in the present.[101] Hsu's constellated connections with QTAPI ancestors are a mode of coalition building that secures QTAPI space in the present and future. Their readings "reconceptualize ancestry" (for QTAPI, whose sense of that term has been populated by "stories often used to essentialize Asian or Asian American identities and cultures") "as an array of stories through which QTAPI place themselves in longer traditions of resistance, courage, and care." Such connections present trans and queer kinship across time as a source of interdependent and "collaborative resilience," through which trans people construct futurity. Trans history is not about proving that trans people are, or have been, "real," or even (only) about demonstrating trans viability for other trans people, but about coalition building for the promise of better futures in the present.

Constellations are culturally and communally embedded: "Each constellation is only one possible configuration among infinite permutations, but it draws meaning from the connections we agree upon."[102] So the histories, presents, and futures that star-literate Nishnaabeg read in any given constellation will be different from those read by other nations or those recalled by classical Greek or Roman mythology. The narratives that Hsu constellates are embedded in, and invested in creating, community. Like Eric Darnell Pritchard before them, Hsu's constellations of transtemporal kinship

99 Simpson, *As We Have Always Done*, 213.

100 Simpson, *As We Have Always Done*, 173. For Simpson's understanding of ancestral time, see, for example, *As We Have Always Done*, 6–10.

101 See Pearce, *Understand Trans Health*, 119–55. The same strategy of anticipation is also used as a mode of protection against disappointment and negative experiences. Trans temporal anticipation is never solely positive.

102 Hsu, *Constellating Home*, 11.

constitute a form of world-building in the mould of Muñoz's vision of queerness as "an insistence on potentiality or concrete possibility for another world."[103] In indigenous thought, ancestral constellations orient toward fugitivity: the refusal of colonial logics of statecraft and the process of rebuilding an alternative existence outside of those structures. For manuscript studies, different reorientations are at stake: yes, of the method and direction of textual criticism and material studies as highlighted by this chapter; but (more importantly) of the provision of space for trans operators through meaningful communal connection to historic trans experience that provides homes in the present future of the field.

This chapter sets up constellation as a trans tactic for navigating the cisheteropatriarchal structures still used in manuscript studies and textual criticism to organize our understanding of manuscript relations. It proposes that other ways of organizing our objects of study are possible, and that such models can offer ways to de-prioritize white supremacist, cisheterosexist modes of canon formation and material analysis, in favour of situated processual networks of communal relations. These networks—rhizomic, constellatory—offer a messier, more realistic model of the materially inflected reality of manuscript production and consumption (and all the positions in between.) As a corollary of that observation, we might consider that constellation was already happening among manuscript producers. For example, in the case of Jean d'Angoulême, who became aware of other copies of the *Canterbury Tales* through which to correct, extend, or adapt his own manuscript. As a dissident tactic for negotiating oppressive structures, constellating manuscripts and other cultural forces was available to medieval trans and queer subjects. Constellations organized according to trans kinship implicate interdependent transtemporal communities of trans experience, offering a path toward trans futurity. In the chapter that follows, I put this suggestion into practice in two different ways: first, by considering how medieval trans and queer readers might encounter community through their own book use; and second, by suggesting that as modern subjects we might also participate in that community formation.

103 Muñoz, *Cruising Utopia*, 1. See, also, Pritchard, *Fashioning Lives.*

Chapter 4

CONSTELLATING TRANS LEGIBILITY

THE FORM OF the codex is mapped to the form of the body: the book has a head, a tail, and a spine that runs between them. In textbooks and diagrams its structures are often referred to in terms of "anatomy." The skin of the parchment page is identified as a site of particular bodily recognition, never fully divorced from its animal origins. Joints, folds, and areas of loose skin are recalled by variations in pigmentation, thickness, and texture.[1] As Sarah Kay demonstrates, book producers could use flaws and irregularities in the parchment surface to extend and augment narrative incidents. For example, in a mid-fourteenth-century copy of Jean de Vignay's *Légende dorée*, a French translation of the Latin *Legenda aurea*, "a tear that has been largely stitched up" is visible to readers of the life of St. Bartholomew, creating "a short-circuit between textual content and the material state of the page" as the parchment becomes a "metaphorical expression[…] of that same, (flayed) human skin."[2] In such instances, the surface is recruited in service of the text: irregularities in the parchment enact the events of the text on the page. In this chapter, I propose that the effect of the parchment skin does not end in its service to particular texts, as a visual-tactile metaphor for the narrative body. Instead, I examine the parchment surface as reading support, which, through its metonymic relationship with (gender)queer bodies, supports the development of trans communities of intimate care.

The surface of the page has become a productive site of study. Surface studies, Georgina Wilson explains, "[m]oves away from a binary of objective/subjective readings" to combine "[m]odels of figurative and material surfaces" as a means of "engag[ing] with the intellectual, political, and emotive responses available to readers."[3] The paper page, Jonathan Senchyne posits, has layers: "the material (paper is made up of cellulose fibers meshed together), the representational (words and images on paper invite

---

1 See, for example, Bischoff, *Urkundenformate*, esp. 48–51; Gumbert, "Skins, Sheets, and Quires," 82–84.

2 Kay, "Original Skin," 55 and 36, and Kay, *Animal Skins*, 89 respectively.

3 Wilson, "Surface Reading Paper," 370 and 371.

interpretation), and the 'presence layer' (the traces of individuals who have contributed to its making)."[4] But paper also has depths. Wilson's study reads through its layers "both materially and metaphorically" in order to "make…room for a greater network of individuals, including women, who intervened in early modern texts."[5] Taking watermarks as "an intellectual prompt," Wilson uses the labour of female rag-pickers to enliven the vertical and horizontal political hierarchies that underpin Ben Johnson's *Sejanus*, to "reintegrate the work of marginalized papermakers into the shaping of literary forms and so to extend literary production beyond its usual gendered and socioeconomic coordinates."[6] Rag paper is also the focus of Orietta Da Rold's *Paper in Medieval England*, which analyzes how medieval English writers and readers responded to the material affordances and cultural implications of this new-to-them technology. Paper's qualities (of "chromaticity," "plasticity," and "porosity and tensility"), Da Rold finds, were not only vital to an increasingly bureaucratic writing culture, and to the promulgation of printing in the following century. Paper production and trade infused (and became highly visible in) the literary imagination as a metaphor that opened up—as Wilson also shows—the multiple levels on which it signalled to contemporary audiences.[7] Similarly, Joshua Calhoun has shown that early modern paper retains "legible ecologies that record the environmental negotiations of people and things, of humans, humanists, and nonhumans."[8] Like its material affordances, these ecological traces (in the form of plant material, gelatine sizing, insects, mould, and decay), enter into the literary imagination "alter[ing] the ways human ideas can be expressed and even conceived."[9] As Senchyne puts it, the paper page "absorbs traces of people, places, and actions, making them available for thinking and touching."[10] In this chapter, I suggest that the parchment surface is also a deep surface that can sustain and transmit touch as trace in the service of communal and intellectual relations.

I have written elsewhere about the potential for the materials of the book to develop and sustain communal networks across geographic and

4 Wilson, "Surface Reading Paper," 370, citing Senchyne, *Intimacy of Paper*, 5.

5 Wilson, "Surface Reading Paper," 370 and 372.

6 Wilson, "Surface Reading Paper," 379 and 376.

7 Da Rold, *Paper in Medieval England*, esp. 180–209.

8 Calhoun, *Nature of the Page*, 1.

9 Calhoun, *Nature of the Page*, 2.

10 Senchyne, *Intimacy of Paper*, 19.

temporal removes.[11] I revisit that argument here, through the model of the constellation developed in the previous chapter. For trans community members, such constellations rely on the trans legibility of material components. Equally, readers must be trans literate: able to identify, decode, and activate features that suggest transness. That a textual object is trans legible, does not mean that every reader will recognize transness in it. As Sarah Pyke and Malcolm Noble observe, queer and trans literacies remain vital to sustaining both individual and communal identities.[12] Queer and trans readers find affinities with and in books, often from a very young age. "It's amazing," Lee Lynch writes in "Cruising the Libraries," "how unerring a kid with a variant eye can be."[13] Through cover copy, card catalogues, and morsels in reviews and conversations, queer and trans readers like Lynch develop "an instinct" for the "literary whisper(s)" that might offer community connection.[14] Such whispers may be materially, as well as textually, instantiated, as in Detroit in 1957, when Kathleen V. Forrest found that she "did not need to look at the title for clues" to the content of the lesbian pulp fiction that "leaped out at [her] from the drugstore rack."[15] In this chapter, I suggest that trans legibility and the concomitant trans literacies developed by gender non-conforming readers predate the card catalogue and the dime novel. I extend work on the parchment page as interface and on the imagery of Christ's side wound to develop an understanding of the surfaces of the medieval book as sites of trans(community)formation through constellation.

Skin Surfaces

In a thirteenth-century English copy of the *Bestiary* of Guillaume le Clerc, Sarah Kay observes a "long hole," which interrupts the description of the weasel. In the bestiary tradition, the weasel is characterized by her unusual reproductive practice: in this version of the text, she is said to conceive through her mouth and give birth through her ear. In Guillaume le Clerc's allegorical reading of the bestiary, the weasel's behaviour is that of the believer who listens to everything they are told but does not retain it. The hole in the page "falls right below the passage…about the Weasel's reproduction,"

11 Sargan, "Trans Codicology."

12 Noble and Pyke, "Queer Bibliography," 154–56.

13 Lynch, "Cruising the Libraries," 6.

14 Lynch, "Cruising the Libraries," 9.

15 Forrest, *Lesbian Pulp Fiction*.

producing on the page a "literal manifestation of her problematic orifices."[16] This alignment of surface and text is one example that Kay provides of parchment chosen as a "material correlate" to narrative.[17] The colocation of text and material, Kay proposes, enhances le Clerc's moralization through jarring bodily recognition. In other words, flaws in the parchment surface draw attention to its status as vulnerable skin, and thereby its ontological likeness to the skin of the human body (which this text reminds us is spiritually, as well as physically, vulnerable). Through the scribe's material choices, the reader is encouraged to "assume" the skin of the weasel/page at any given narrative moment.[18]

Some manuscript makers more directly evoke the human body. Nancy Vine Durling reads five holes in a page used to transcribe lyrics from the Passion group in British Library, MS Harley 2253 as "a kind of analogue to Christ's own wounded body."[19] The surface of the page thus provides a material aid to the contemplation demanded by the text. But Christ's body also presents a mechanic to understand the skin of the book outside of the narrative moment. The middle English *Charters of Christ* tradition consists of a series of texts that imagine Christ's promise of salvation granted in the form of a document written upon the crucified body:

> And so I stood bounde all the nyght
> Tyll on the morowe þat was light
> Streyned well faste vp-on a tree
> As parchemyn owyth for to be
> Heryth nowe & ʒe shall wetyn
> Howe thys chartyr was I-wretyn
> Ouer al my face fell the ynke
> Thornys in myn hed be-gonne to synke
> The pennys þat the letterys wretyn
> Were scorges þat I was wytht smetyn...[20]

In this case, the features of the parchment document or page are mapped on to Christ's body:[21] Christ's skin, the properly prepared parchment; his blood, "the ynke"; his wounds, "the letterys"; and the "scorges" used upon

16 Kay, *Animal Skins*, 84.

17 Kay, *Animal Skins*, 86.

18 Kay, *Animal Skins*, 151.

19 Durling, "British Library MS Harley 2253," 291.

20 Holsinger, *On Parchment*, 219n43.

21 Holsinger, *On Parchment*, 219.

Figure 9. *The Short Charter of Christ*, an illustrated Yorkshire Carthusian religious miscellany, fifteenth century. London, British Library, MS Additional 37049, fol. 23r. Reproduced by permission of the British Library.

him, the "pennys (pens)." An illustrated copy of the short Charter, copied in a Carthusian miscellany in the second half of the fifteenth century, depicts Christ before the cross, presenting the charter that holds the text in his still nailed hands (Figure 9).[22] The text is unlineated and the copy bordered to represent a flat folio, with a wax seal hanging from the bottom, emphasizing its documentary status. Christ bleeds profusely, with the blood picked up in the red tipped initials that mark the start of each poetic line. The parchment surface has been left uncoloured to represent both the body and the document, again suggesting that the body of Christ, the copy we hold, and the one described are "co-extensive." The implication is that this copy in this book can be understood as metonymic for some hypothetical original charter and so participates in the materiality of Christ's body.

The idea of Christ's body as "incarnate writing" is not unfamiliar. The opening of the Gospel of John reads, "In principio erat Verbum, et Verbum erat apud Deum, et Deus erat Verbum. (In the beginning there was the word, and the word was with God, and the word was God.)"[23] Sarah Noonan, Eleanor Baker, and Bruce Holsinger trace this colocation of page and (divine) skin in written and illustrated traditions.[24] Such metaphors evoke the form of the book and the manual labour that brought it into being, the status of the book as a devotional locus, and the affective processes that govern reading practice. As Baker demonstrates, in Middle English literature the pervasive use of bodily metaphors, like those found in the *Charters of Christ*, evidence a "widespread familiarity" with the ontological code-switching—between parchment, skin, and human body—that they entail.[25] Holsinger observes, after surveying images of Christ as book found in fifteenth-century books of hours, "a long tradition of bookish thought that associated human skin intimately with the carnality and materiality of writing in its sacrificial immediacy...*The Book of Nature*, the *Book of the Heart*, the *Charter of Christ*: these and other topoi draw on the technology and physicality of parchment to conceive membrane books and documents as a symbol, figure, or totem central to the ritual and theological lives of the human subjects who read, touch, and consume them. As the Word of God, the book of skin embodies the sacrificial dimensions of Christian redemption while inducing others to

22 London, British Library, MS Additional 37049 (Short *Charter of Christ*), fol. 23r.

23 Jn 1:1 LV (DR)

24 Noonan, "Bodies of Parchment"; Baker, "References to Material Texts"; Holsinger, *On Parchment*, 193–222.

25 Baker, "References to Material Texts," 168.

participate through their own scriptive identifications in the great incarnate narrative."[26]

Richard de Bury's *Philobiblon* (1345) is peopled by books. De Bury's books speak in the first person—"we who are the light of faithful souls everywhere"—and take verbs usually reserved for living creatures: they have "slumbered through long ages...wake up and are astonished."[27] As Michael Camille has observed, it is in books' fleshly capacities that de Bury is most invested.[28] For de Bury, books are sensual and responsive. As they age, de Bury's books suffer bodily infirmities: back pain, "palsy," and "bleared eyes."[29] In their sickness they are fleshy too; their illness likened to those of "Lazarus[...] and Job," both of whom were associated with diseases of the skin. Camille points out the capacity for iconographic connections between the afflictions of these figures and the "tears and sores that disfigure parchment."[30] However, no actual sores are needed to activate the connection. The invocation of the material of the book is enough to make the "flesh of the volumes" both substitute and metonym for the (saintly) human body.[31]

This is not to imply that medieval readers saw *every* book as a living object and *every* parchment page as potential human skin. Conservator Nancy K. Turner has warned against foreclosing medieval understandings of parchment's materiality. She reminds us that parchment is a "manufactured material" with "varying qualities, features, and uses," and that medieval readers had a different "knowledge and understanding of the material" than we do today.[32] Kay also worries about attributing anachronistic standards to medieval readers perceptions of the skin of the page. Peggy McCracken finds that animal skins were "a technology of sovereignty" in medieval culture, the wearing of which "reinstates human dominion over animals as well as

26 Holsinger, *On Parchment*, 211.

27 de Bury, *Philobiblon*, iv.72 and viii.120.

28 Camille, "Book as Flesh."

29 de Bury, *Philobiblon*, iv.62–64: see Camille, "Book as Flesh," 54.

30 Camille, "Book as Flesh," 54.

31 Camille, "Book as Flesh," 55.

32 Turner, "Materiality of Medieval Parchment," 41. Turner's intervention is tremendously useful, and I engage with it more extensively in my forthcoming monograph, *Reading Early Middle English Books*. However, it is worth noting, as Baker does of the texts she surveys, that many material metaphors required an understanding of *both* the dermal origins of parchment and the techniques by which it was processed: see, for example, the *Charters of Christ* tradition above: Baker, "References to Material Texts," 50–79.

over land and other human subjects."[33] It is natural that the "sovereignty" people felt over the animals they raised or hunted should be extended to the products they made from their hides also. From this perspective, the parchment page says less about the human body than it does about the workings of social and environmental power. Indeed, proto-capitalist values of ownership might raise the status of the processed skin as written object, especially as it became associated with the institutions of political, legal, and/or religious institutions as the bearer of normative text. Here, the processed parchment skin signals dominion over not just animals but people too.

At the outset, the alignment of parchment pages with trans bodies might seem simplistic and even a little crass. Comparisons involving shaving, stitching, and scarring write themselves, evoking a medicalized idea of transness that echoes the pernicious and nonsensical concept of "*the* surgery"—the false idea that gender reassignment is achieved through a single (usually non-specific) surgery and that until this has happened transition is invalid or unattainable ("But have you had *the* surgery?"). Such concerns notwithstanding, the skin is a complex and multivalent site for trans people: it can feel wrong, or uncomfortable, it might be surgically or hormonally altered, but it can also be reformed, decorated, celebrated, a site of affirmation and being in the world. Scars are not just the still-tender memories of old wounds, for many they are affirmative indicators of survival and becoming. Trans skin may be all or none of these things; it may be a mark of shame and/or a source of joy. The skin, Sue Cataldi concludes in her book *Emotion, Depth, and Flesh*, both "protects us from others and exposes us to them," but for many trans people exposure risks judgement, censorship, or violence.[34] In either scenario, trans skin is a site of hyperawareness, a surface that is policed and surveilled by the self and others.

It is not wrong, then, to suggest that for some the marks on the parchment page—holes, sewn repairs, surface abrasions, and beneath them bruises, pores, and vasculature—prompt recognition. "The transsexual body," Susan Stryker writes, in the performance piece "My Words to Victor Frankenstein above the Village of Chamounix," "is a technological construction. It is flesh torn apart and sewn together again in a shape other than that in which it was born."[35] Hyperbole is intended in Stryker's monologue, which in 1994 sought to reclaim trans experience from the normativizing

33 McCracken, *Skin of the Beast*, 9.

34 Cataldi, *Emotion, Depth, and Flesh*, 145.

35 Stryker, "My Words to Victor Frankenstein," 238.

aims of the medical establishment, but it reflects the truth of some trans experience. And, as Gabrielle M. W. Bychowski and Turner have variously shown, the parchment page is a surface that has undergone a transition: the transition from skin, to parchment, to page is not a gender transition, "but what emerges from reading both skins for trans textuality is an affirmation that within all surfaces lie depths of ongoing transition."[36] In considering the affinities between the body and the page, then, we must think beyond simple equivalences and celebrate the complexity of trans bodily experience.

Like reading, as Turner and Kay point out, the surface is culturally, socially, and historically embedded and not all signs are equally legible to all readers. With the terms trans literacy and trans legibility, I intend to flag not just the historical and cultural contingency of reading practice (broadly construed as the interpretation of signs), but also its embodied individual exigencies. The widespread deployment of the parchment page both as bodily metaphor and as staging space for embodied action shows that connection with the skin-ness of the page was possible. Trans and gender non-conforming readers, I suggest in this chapter, may be particularly alive to the skin of the surface.

Trans Pages in Normative Books

When Bychowski observes the ontological overlaps between the trans body and the medieval page, which she formulates in terms of "trans textuality," she outlines three principles by which moments of affinity between the two might be understood: "dysphoria, duration, depth."[37] In what follows, I take Bychowski's principles as a starting point from which to expand as I shift from the consideration of parchment as subservient to text in the creation of meaning (as writing support) to an understanding of its material properties as a world-building skin-technology in its own right. I begin by extending the modes of recognition discussed above to the trans body in particular, through bibliographic images of the wounds of Christ. The devotional books that contain such images tend to be highly normative, though not necessarily in the same way as the legal rolls and ledgers discussed in Chapter 2. Books of hours, in particular, are a common venue. While such books could be personalized through the selection of "accessory texts" and the addition of prayers, images, and personal details, they required a standard set

36 Bychowski, "Trans Textuality," 322.

37 Bychowski, "Trans Textuality," 321–25.

of materials.[38] Devotional books, especially ones like these that offered lay readers "a means by which they could participate for themselves in the daily round of prayer and worship that typified the lives of monks and priests," are heavily imbricated in the religio-cultural structures that enforce compulsory cisheterosexuality.[39] The book of hours is exemplary of the way the late medieval church developed mechanics to regulate the routines of the laity. It became important to regulating the religious lives of those with the means to afford them by standardizing (up to a point) the materials, routines, and observances that structured the secular year. But at the same time, it provided separation between lay parishioners and monastic practice (a different book, a limited access), retaining space within the institutions of the church for other configurations of sex and gender.

Images of Christ's side wound appeared regularly in devotional contexts from the early fourteenth century. Increased interest in Christ's wounds as symbols of suffering and sacrifice at the Crucifixion is marked by the appearance of masses dedicated to the wounds in missals and private prayer books.[40] A stylized imagery of the side wound developed, in which the wound was abstracted from the body, and reoriented vertically within a diamond, lozenge, marquise, or teardrop-shaped frame. In some examples, such as the full-page miniature pasted into the Bohun Hours, the wound appears alongside the Arma Christi, a depiction of the Crucifixion, or both.[41]

Devotion to the side wound was one aspect of a broader theological interest in Christ as a figure who could transcend gender. Julian of Norwich's conception of Trinitarian theology places Christ in the position of "our very Moder":

> I understode three manner of beholdyng of Moderhede in God. The first is groundid of our kinde makeying. The second is taken of our kinde, and there begynnyth the Moderhede of grace. The thrid is Moderhede of werkyng, and therin is a forthspreadyng, be the same grace, of length, and bredth, and of heyth, and of depenes withouten end - and al His own luf.[42]

Julian inherits this understanding from a tradition that associated Christ with motherhood via the feminine-coded values of nurture, sacrifice, and

38 For a brief overview of the genre, see Clemens and Graham, *Introduction to Manuscript Studies*, 208–21. On their adaptability to owner's wishes, in particular, see especially Rudy, *Piety in Pieces*; Rudy, *Postcards on Parchment*.

39 Clemens and Graham, *Introduction to Manuscript Studies*, 208.

40 See Rubin, *Corpus Christi*.

41 Oxford, Bodleian Library, MS Auct. D.4.4 (Bohun Hours), fol. 236v.

42 Julian of Norwich, *Shewings*, LIX, lines 2470 and 2474–78.

unconditional love. Liz Herbert McAvoy views this moment of Christological explication as the culmination of a "feminization of Christ's body" that acts—through juxtaposition, identification, and dislocation—as a "matrix" for Julian's *Revelations*.[43] Julian's Christology is "fully embodied" when she witnesses the Crucifixion in a vision. Here, she presents Christ in a perpetual state of labour, out of which comes salvation, through the shedding of "full thick," "browne rede" menstrual blood and then the accelerated "bright rede" flow of post-partum hemorrhaging.[44]

In her 1982 monograph *Jesus as Mother*, Caroline Walker Bynum assesses the tradition developed by women from twelfth-century Cistercian writings that showed an "increasing preference for analogies taken from human relationships."[45] Such preferences included allusions to other familial relations, community leaders, and friends, as well as to the special care provided by mothers. Contemporary medicine understood that a mother's milk was produced from her blood, and idealized mothers nursing their own children, so the conflation of Christ's side wound (from which flowed blood and water: John 19:33–34) with the maternal breast was "more than merely the parallelism of two bodily fluids."[46] Thus wrote Aelred of Rievaulx in the early twelfth century: "Then one of the soldiers opened his side with a lance and there came forth blood and water. Hasten, linger not, eat the honeycomb with your honey, drink your wine with your milk. The blood is changed into wine to gladden you, the water into milk to nourish you."[47] The use of bodily imagery was intensified by women like Julian's predecessors, Gertrude the Great and Mechthild of Magdeburg, both nuns of the Cistercian-influenced house at Helfta, who used "graphic gynocentric imagery" to explain the mysteries of the Sacred Heart.[48] Mechthild of Magdeburg dwells on the eroticism of the soul's relationship with God, writing "He kisses her (the soul) passionately with his divine mouth...Then she rises to the heights of bliss and

---

43 McAvoy, "Moders Service," 184.

44 See McAvoy, "Moders Service," 193 and 189. The Carthusian prioress, Marguerite of Oingt, is more explicit in her figuration of the Crucifixion as a birth scene as she describes Christ labouring on the bed of the cross, before he "gave birth to the whole world": see Easton, "Wound of Christ," 401.

45 Bynum, *Jesus as Mother*, 129, for example.

46 Bynum, *Jesus as Mother*, 132.

47 Aelred of Rievaulx, *Treatises*, 90–91.

48 McAvoy, "Moders Service," 181. For more background on the convent at Helfta see Bynum, *Jesus as Mother*, 174–81.

to the most exquisite pain when she becomes truly intimate with him.[49] The side wound in particular could be kissed, licked, touched, and drunk from in gestures that might be read as both erotic and intimately nourishing.

Until recently, scholars could be rather coy in noticing the alignment between the shape of the stylized wound images and that of the vulva. However, in the last twenty years the likeness has been more readily accepted: Martha Easton describes the images as "almost inescapably vaginal."[50] The metonymy is encoded in James of Milan's *Stimulus amoris* (1293), where James puns on the proximity of the words *vulna* (wound) and *vulva*:

> O amantissima vulnera Domini mei Iesu Christi! Nam, cum ea quadam vice oculis subintraem apertis...ibi tanta abundo dulcedine, ut tibi non valeam onarrare. Et qui prius pro peccatoribus fuerat in utero virginali, nune dignatur me miserum inter sua viscera comportare...quantumcumque me pariat, scio, quod semper sua vulnera sunt aperta, et per ea in eius uterum iterum introibo.
>
> (Oh most loving wounds of my Lord Jesus Christ! For, when I enter into it with my eyes open...there I abound with such sweetness that I cannot tell you. And He who was previously in the Virgin's womb for sinners, now deigns to carry me, wretched, within his bowels...No matter how often he births me, I know that his wounds are always open, and through them I will enter his womb again.)[51]

The connection is reinforced by the makers of medieval manuscripts: significantly, when it comes to the gendering of Christ, in several thirteenth-century depictions of the Crucifixion that show St. Peter/God assisting in the birth of the figure of Holy Church—dressed in robes and crown—who emerges from the wound in Christ's side.[52] A thirteenth-century Parisian *Bible moralisée* interestingly parallels this sacrificial birth to the creation of Eve, depicting her being birthed, fully-formed, out of Adam's side in the roundel above and casting God in the role of midwife in both cases (Figure 10).

Images of the wound were often purported to be life-size and sometimes commentary was provided to assert this claim. A fifteenth-century

49 Mechthild of Magdeburg, *Flowing Light*, 88–89.

50 Easton, "Wound of Christ," 397. See also observations by Trexler, "Gendering Jesus Crucified," 109; Lewis, "Wound in Christ's Side"; and Lochrie, "Mystical Acts, Queer Tendencies."

51 James of Milan, *Stimulus amoris*, 70–71 (for more, see 70–76); see Lochrie, "Mystical Acts, Queer Tendencies," 189–90.

52 See Lewis, "Wound in Christ's Side," 215; Sexton, "Gender-Queerying Christ's Wounds."

Figure 10. Detail from a *Bible moralisée*, Paris, 1225–1250. Vienna, Österreichische Nationalbibliothek, MS Cod. 2554, fol. 1v. Courtesy of the Austrian National Library's open access initiative, https://data.onb.ac.at/rep/10017A6C.

Figure 11. An image of Christ's side wound added to the Lewkenor Hours on a sewn-in slip, England, 1375–1400. London, Lambeth Palace Library, MS 545, fol. 78v. Reproduced by permission of the Lambeth Palace Library on behalf of the Archbishop of Canterbury.

illustration of Christ's side wound stitched into the English Lewkenor Hours, is both abstracted from Christ's body—floating in space within an immediate rhombic frame, itself centred on a larger framed black square—and mapped closely onto it (Figure 11).[53] The double-framing of the image contains its potential for bodily messiness and draws attention to its status as artistic representation. However, the writing inside the first frame, which proclaims that the image is "[t]he mesur*e* of þ*e* wonde of our*e* lorde ihe*su* crist," asserts its proximity to a real and measurable wound. As Bynum

53 London, Lambeth Palace Library, MS 545 (Lewkenor Hours), fol. 78v.

documents, the production of wound images "to the dimensions supposedly given in a vision or brought from the Holy Land" asserted their metonymy *with* Christ's body. Metric relics, which claimed to replicate the length, or a portion of the length, of a devotional object, body, or place, were increasingly popular in the fourteenth century as "metonymy or concomitance became a general way of thinking about presence."[54] In this context, images of the wound reflect the logic of material relics, like a vial of Thomas Becket's blood or the preserved finger of John the Baptist, in which the fragmented body invokes and transmits the power of the whole. In some ways, then, this wound presents a body outside of gender—a body that is wound only; but in others, it is all gender—insomuch as we might measure that attribute through the primary sex characteristics of the vulvic wound.

The wound in the Lewkenor Hours might be compared with a similar image in a passional made in the early fourteenth century for Kunigunde, the Abbess of the Benedictine convent of St. George's in Prague Castle, by a canon of that house. Two full page miniatures in the manuscript show different visualizations of the *arma christi*: in the first, they take the form of heraldic insignia displayed on a shield; in the second, the instruments of the crucifixion along with a life-size wound, surround Christ as Man of Sorrows (Figure 12).[55] In this context, the side wound is not abstracted from Christ's body but an extension of it, painted hovering above his hand as if magnified. The doubling of the wound on the page emphasizes the synecdochic qualities of such images, in which all versions are one and the same wound. Importantly, these two examples demonstrate that the visual rhetoric of the side wound was shared across secular and institutional contexts.

Rather than a "vulvar synecdoche that feminizes the body," Sexton argues, "the vulva-wound is better understood as evidence of the integral fluidity of Christ's gender, being incorporated into a body that refuses to signify as either/or within binary terms."[56] As such, Christ's wound becomes a model of trans potential within normative devotional contexts. Placed within books, the transcendent possibilities of Christ's wound combine with the metonymic affordances of the parchment page, activating the volume as a site of gender possibility. Here, the transitivity of Christ's body is extended

54 Bynum, "Violent Imagery," 23.

55 Prague, National Library of the Czech Republic, MS XIV.A.17 (Abbess Kunigund's Passional), fols. 3r and 10r. For more on the composition of the manuscript see Lewis "Wound in Christ's Side," 204–5.

56 Sexton, "Gender-Queerying Christ's Wounds," 139.

to the material of the page: as in the examples of the previous section, the book also provides a space for Christ's body to be realized.

It is worth repeating that such perceptions are culturally, socially, and historically situated. Not everyone who came into contact with images of the side wound would read them gynecologically or, if they did, extend that gynecological reading to their gendered vision of Christ. However, the traditions outlined above demonstrate that such readings were available. Similarly, our perception of the medieval gendering of Christ is situated. I approach these images from a trans and queer perspective, in which both of those terms are used to express a wide range of non-specific behaviours and identifications that resist normative structures of cisheterosexist power. These transcendent images of divine gender occupy a troubling position within such claims to resistance because of their transmission within such arguably normativizing books. However, this chapter argues that their place within such books reorients the cisheterosexist and patriarchal structures of the church (as represented by the book of hours), tactically turning normative models toward embodied trans experience and community building through the constellating affordances of trans touch. Moreover, the replication of such images in institutional and lay contexts, and the potential for personal selection by book owners, sets them in constellation, facilitating trans "lines of flight" into and around monastic gender-flexible space.

Taking seriously the two suggestions made above—the first that the parchment page might, with the right textual and/or environmental cues, invoke the presence of human skin; the second, that images of the side wound in both secular and monastic contexts participate in a tradition of Christ as gender transcendent figure—I suggest that, in these devotional and medico-devotional contexts, parchment pages that bear wound images might be imagined as a trans skin technology. Here, the colocation of codicological (parchment), spiritual (Christ's), and reading skins found in the *Charters of Christ* and other similar traditions, has (trans)gendered implications. Through the imposition of the "vaginal" side wound, the body of Christ is transposed from a neutral (masculine) body to a gender transcendent one. Further, in its abstraction from Christ's body, the wound is superimposed onto a new body, that of the reader. The presence of the wound on the surface(?) of the parchment skin/reading skin, offers further (trans)gender possibilities for readers and users.

Constellating Trans Touch through the Page

In the final sections of this chapter, I propose that the gender transcendent possibilities of images of the side wound, as they are inscribed on the parchment page, offer up a tactic for the formation of trans communities of care across and within normative book objects. In parchment, I find a skin technology that can hold and sustain trans touch. In doing so, I build on the significance of Sexton's observation that haptic interaction with images of the wound could provide a source of gender and gendered recognition, identification, and becoming.[57] I observe in such touches the gestures of intimate, sometimes erotic, gender labour and care. These gestures, I suggest, when retained by the page, form constellated communities of trans carers across image networks.

My first claim, that parchment registers, holds, and transmits touch, is based on the understanding that parchment is a deep surface. The skin, Sara Ahmed and Jackie Stacey show in the introduction to the volume *Thinking Through the Skin* (2003), has been fetishized as a "boundary-object" that separates the body from the world around it. It is a legible surface or interface "assumed to contain either the body, identity, well-being or value"; "allow[...] the contours of the body to appear *as given*"; and transmit the truth of what is within outward.[58] On this basis, parchment presents an ideal instantiation of skin as surface. It is a thin, flexible substrate, on which meaning is transmitted unmediated in the form of writing. However, neither parchment nor skin uncritically transmits the truth. Just as writing is a cultural product, the meanings attributed to skin are culturally produced. Nor do those meanings remain on the surface. As Ahmed, Stacey, and others have argued, the skin is not without depth. Trans men have an acute sense of the skin's physical depth: a subcutaneous testosterone injection is best given with a 5/8" needle held at 90° or a 1" needle held at 45°. Just as Wilson takes watermarks as a testament "to the depths of paper," Bychowski considers the pores visible on the parchment page as evidence of the skin's depths.[59] These pores, she suggests, reveal that the bodies that Chaucer's Physician "works to seal off" in his tale are actually "penetrated and porous," evidencing "internal touch, anima, active desire, and shame."[60]

57 Sexton, "Gender-Queerying Christ's Wounds," 146–50.

58 Ahmed and Stacey, "Dermographies," 3, emphasis mine.

59 See Wilson, "Surface Reading Paper," 373.

60 Bychowski, "Trans Textuality," 329.

Images of the side wound present another means of accessing the skin's depths. Visually, the black interior of the wound implies an unseen, unknowable depth to the depiction: a "void."[61] As Olsen demonstrates, that "void" was visualized by medieval devotants as variably extensive. In Olsen's words, the wound was a "liminal space or gateway that signified the transition between secular space (the here and now of the beholder) and sacred space (salvation and life-everlasting)."[62] The wound, per James of Milan, offered a location that could be entered into as part of devotional performance.

For Gilles Deleuze, the wound might be considered fold-like. "[F]olds" like this are indicative of the skin's bodily function; it performs "a folding-in of external influences and a simultaneous unfolding outwards of affects."[63] Deleuze's theorization accords with Olsen's description of the performative wound, which effects a similar folding in and folding out as it "simultaneously performed for the believer (it bled) or was acted upon through tactile interaction (touching or kissing), thereby inviting participation on the part of the devotee."[64] Didier Anzieu conceptualizes the psychical apparatus in similarly topographical terms, where the skin presents a multilayered, flexible "surface containing pouches and cavities," which offers a protective but permeable boundary between the internal Ego and external stimuli. The skin, Anzieu proposes, is "a filter of exchanges and for the recording of the earliest traces, the function that makes representation possible."[65] By either formulation, the skin is not a flat surface that simply receives or permits inscription, but a deep and textured surface that changes and is changed by our experience of the world.

Reading a manuscript (and, to some degree, any material book) is an intensely embodied experience. In parchment codices, the feel, sound, and smell of the page all contribute to the reading experience and participate in the delivery of information. Medieval interactions with books were accompanied by embodied gestural practices, variously interpreted by modern scholars: from the vocalization and sub-lingual muttering that Paul Saenger suggests accompanied reading into the fifteenth century, to the fetishistic

61 Olsen, "Penetrating the Void."

62 Olsen, "Penetrating the Void," 315.

63 See Braidotti, "Teratologies," 159, as cited by Ahmed and Stacey, "Dermographies," 4.

64 Olsen, "Penetrating the Void," 315.

65 Anzieu, *Skin-Ego*, 112 and 105 respectively.

grooming and preening of the collector.[66] In recent years, touch has been accorded a more significant role in the medieval reading process. Kathryn M. Rudy observes a range of "deliberate and charged" touching techniques indicative of different affective responses to manuscript imagery and content. The damage produced by routine and/or extraordinary touch, she suggests, can "reveal how books were handled," and in so doing inform us of what was important to their individual or communal users.[67] For Andrew James Johnston, Wolfram R. Keller and Henry Ravenhall, medieval readers' impulse to touch reveals that "manuscripts operated as an interface that allowed [them], through certain acts of (self-)inscription, to situate themselves politically, ethically, and emotionally in relation to" textual content.[68] In my own work, I figure touch as opening up a suite of embodied reading practices that locate the page as a social space for bodily community formation.[69] In each case, haptic approaches to the page result in what Camille terms the "interpenetration of corporeality and codicology."[70]

Images of the side wound present a particular instance of that interpenetration. Sexton analyzes an image of the five wounds of Christ in the Loftie Hours, a mid-fifteenth-century Dutch prayerbook equipped with a schema of eighteen miniatures by the Masters of the Delft Grisailles, that show evidence of having been subject to what Rudy categorizes as "wet touch."[71] The image displays the five wounds in red, oriented vertically, organized two by two with a larger wound in the centre and with copious amounts of dripping blood. The ink of the bottom two wounds has been blurred by repeated touching, which seems to have lifted the red ink from the centre of each.[72] Wet touch, Rudy shows, is often a sign of veneration. It might include kissing, either with the mouth against the manuscript, or with the finger(s) as intermediary; weeping; or the application of some kind of sanctified substance

66 See, Saenger, *Space Between Words*; Camille, "Book as Flesh." Other studies have taken a different view to Saenger. Most notably, Coleman, *Public Reading* emphasizes the persistence of reading aloud in the form of communal reading and performance (although I would note that the two are not mutually exclusive.)

67 Rudy, *Touching Parchment*, 2:4.

68 Johnston, Keller, and Ravenhall, "Touching Troy," 425.

69 Sargan, "Trans Codicology," 578–82. For more on this, see my forthcoming book: Sargan, *Reading Early Middle English*.

70 Camille, "Book as Flesh," 36.

71 Rudy, "Touching the Book Again." See also, Rudy, *Touching Parchment*.

72 Baltimore, Walters Art Museum, MS W.165 (Loftie Hours), fol. 110v; Sexton, "Gender-Queerying Christ's Wounds," 147.

(like oil or holy water). Wet touches often build up over time as part of a repeated ritual of engagement with the images of the book.[73] Sexton associates users' interactions with the Loftie wounds with Mark Amsler's gestures of "affective literacy," in which meditative and devotional contact with the wound gave readers the "freedom to touch, to feel (literally and emotionally), to become, through meditative practices, similar to [Christ's] suffering body, connected to it through touch and sight."[74]

Rudy identifies wet-touch in another image from Abbess Kunigunde's Passional—the dedication image of the abbess on her dais. Here, the wear is "directed entirely to Kunigunde's face" and appears to have been caused when a reader, or more likely generations of successive readers, "kissed her finger and then touched the represented face with a moistened digit." The marks of the finger(s) can be seen, where the ink from the grid-like pattern of Kunigunde's habit has been transferred to the blank space of the parchment surrounding the face. Rudy points to similar osculatory practices at work during the Mass, when the Missal was kissed by the celebrant performing the *Te igitur* or reading from the gospels. This context, she suggests, implies that Kunigunde was the subject of saint-like veneration by the nuns of her community, who perhaps kissed her image as a regular, ritualized aspect of their reading of the book. Indeed, the marks participate in the ritualization of such actions, their presence punctuating the gestures of reading and acting as prompts for readers to repeat them year on year.[75] In this case, the marks of wet touch are both evidence of community identity and relationality and the facilitators of those connections, inviting others into communal relationships.

The side wound in Kunigunde's Passional was also subject to wet touch. Here, the contact drifts between the wound and the adjacent face of Christ on the cross, marked by a darker area of parchment and a single wet drip mark that has lifted red ink from the wound itself (Figure 12). It is possible that this touching represents a similar kind of mobile devotional veneration, traversing between Christ's face and the wound as generations of users kissed the image. Images of Christ Crucified, Rudy observes, were sometimes equipped with osculatory targets to divert the kisses of celebrants

73 Rudy, "Touching the Book Again," 250–52.

74 Sexton, "Gender-Queerying Christ's Wounds," 147. See Amsler, "Affective Literacies," 98.

75 Rudy, "Touching the Book," 252.

Figure 12. Christ as Man of Sorrows displaying the *Arma Christi* and side wound. In Abbess Kunigunde's Passional, Prague, 1313–1321. Prague, National Library of the Czech Republic, MS XIV.A.17, fol. 10r. Reproduced by permission of the National Library of the Czech Republic.

during the Mass away from Christ's face and/or feet.[76] Perhaps the wound in this image enacted a similar function, allowing the nuns to participate in the moment of transubstantiation by re-enacting the gestures of the Mass. Widespread imagery, particularly among Cistercian communities, of kissing, touching, and drinking from the wound in particular, might also inspire readers to physical touch as a form of devotion.

However, even within these institutional and ritualized settings, the gesture of the kiss should not be divorced from its intimacy and potential eroticism. The kisses offered to Kunigunde's face in the Passional's frontispiece, while they may be devotional, also affirm her status as part of the community. They are an intimate gesture shared between the members of the convent—those present at any given time, those who repeat them across time, and the nuns and abbess depicted in the image—to reaffirm their shared status and values. As such, they are gestures that maintain and direct communal relations. In these material settings, Vebeke Olsen claims, "the wound could be visualized, venerated, touched, partaken of, and even penetrated by the faithful in an infinite variety of fluid scenarios involving the senses and that were freed from the constraints of biblical narrative and time."[77] The kissing of the wound, particularly when its trans potential is recognized, implicates the user in gestures of queer and trans intimacy and "provokes the erotic tension of the *vulna/vulva* overlap."[78]

Other images of the side wound exhibit different kinds of contact from their readers. Scratch marks are visible on the surface of the wound in the Lewkenor Hours (Figure 11). Other examples, like a wound incorporated into a miniature of the Crucifixion thought to be by the Fauvel Master have been rubbed from the page. The wound in an illustrated copy of Gautier de Metz's *Image du monde* produced in Paris in the 1320s is prioritized by its location, overspilling the bounds of its own portal at the centre of the page. The centre of the wound has been "partly erased and the black and red paint rubbed off" through vigorous scratching.[79] Another example, found among a series of prayers on a roll that Mary Morse categorizes as a birth girdle, shows wear and abrasions to the diamond at the centre of the wound.[80]

---

76 Rudy, *Touching Parchment*, vol. 1, 86–108.

77 Olsen, "Penetrating the Void," 323.

78 Amsler, "Affective Literacy," 98.

79 Amsler, "Affective Literacy," 98. See Paris, Bibliothèque nationale de France, MS français 547 (*Image du monde*), fol. 140r.

80 London, British Library, Harley Roll T 11. See Morse, *English Birth Girdles*, 271–300.

Still more images exhibit flaking, chipping, and smudging of paint. Such abrasions indicate that these wounds have been touched vigorously with dry hands, in some cases over long periods. Dry touch and wet touch might be similarly ritualized, with similar affective resonances. But dry touch may also register other kinds of heightened emotional states—like anger, fear, or frustration. Indeed, some readers, like the reader of Gautier de Metz's *Image du monde*, who nearly succeeded in removing the wound from the page altogether, may have been acting out of repulsion rather than devotional interest. As Sexton reminds us, there is no way to know exactly what motivated users to touch their books in this way, but it is clear that depictions of the side wound attracted touch in ways that other images, and even other parts of the same image, did not.[81]

More appealing, perhaps, is the suggestion that, like so many doubting Thomases, readers probed the wound for Christological assurance and gender affirmation. In his analysis of depictions of the crucifixion, Richard C. Trexler figures Christ's body as "a volume to be penetrated by [the] audience."[82] Building on the suggestion that images of the side wound allowed readers to participate in St. Thomas's affirmation of the truth (physical truth, devotional truth, gender truth) of the resurrection, I suggest the readers probing of wound images sets up relational networks of queer and trans questioning, witnessing, and intimacy (erotic or not). Indeed, the vulvic wound might also draw to mind the apocryphal story of Salome, the midwife at the birth of Christ who did not believe in Mary's virginity, so probed her vagina with a finger to feel for the presence of a hymen. By touching the wound, readers witness the truth of Christ's gender transcendent body and participate in the intimate process of caring for that body. Such interactions provide space for queer and trans interrelation and establish communities of intimate care. They do this in two ways: first, through trans skin technologies that allow parchment to register, hold, and transmit touch through time (a concept somewhat aligned with Bychowski's sense of "duration"); second, through the tactic of constellation. Such constellatory tactics invoke Karma Lochrie's observation that the feminizing of Christ's body "opens a mesh of possibilities" for devotional action, but provides that mesh with connective, directional, and liberatory potential.[83]

---

81 Sexton, "Gender-Queerying Christ's Wounds," 147.

82 Trexler, "Gendering Jesus Crucified," 108.

83 Lochrie, "Mystical Acts, Queer Tendencies," 189.

The skin-to-skin contact—skin to page, skin to holy body as page, skin to reader's body as page—that devotional touch effects, then, is retained by the deep surface of the parchment. That contact, variously figured as loving, venerating, questioning, witnessing, is registered on the page, but it also becomes part of the books' affective resonances and affinities. Bychowski frames such affinities as a recognition of the page's (trans) "soul": the skin, she suggests—building on Kay—is "the grounds from which an *animus* (soul) emerges" and that *animus* within the parchment results in recognition that "emerges when skin touches skin, reader touches manuscript."[84] Elsewhere I have articulated similar feelings of connection in more secular terms: "The parchment surface retains trans experiences to be reanimated in concert with trans literate readers."[85] Rudy describes how such touches might build up over time, the marks that they make becoming a cue to further ritualized touching. Deleuze and Guattari extend the social implications of such touches. We understand from them that the inner surfaces of the wound-fold touch back. The surface of the parchment, as a synecdoche for gender transcendent body of Christ, offers spiritual and social affirmation to its users. Finally, the wound offers contact between users, as it sustains the touches of those who have come before. Just as the generations of nuns who touched and kissed the face of Abbess Kunigunde reaffirmed their participation in a shared convent community, successive users of these vulvic wound images shared affective bonds across the surface of the page.

* * *

The affective trans communities developed on the page are not delimited by the boundaries of the book. As I have demonstrated elsewhere, shared codicological structures might be deployed as a mechanism of community formation. For example, the use of seal skin chemises in Cistercian libraries allowed monks in separate houses to participate in a community through shared visual and haptic experiences.[86] I suggest that images of the wound offered similar tactics of community formation. Such images form constellations that can amass trans experience across space and time and put readers into affirming and intimate relation with other users of the gender transcendent wound. In doing so, they afforded those participating in the trans potentials of the side wound access to the single gendered, non-normative

84 Bychowski, "Trans Textuality," 324 and 332.

85 Sargan, "Trans Codicology," 581.

86 See Sargan, "Trans Codicology," 578–80.

spaces of religious houses from a position inside the normative and norm-policing spaces of the book of hours.

When considered in constellation, the locations and formats of wound images provide for their use in the construction of a trans community of care. The earliest examples of the genre, of which Abbess Kunigunde's is one, are found in volumes associated with female religious communities.[87] The images are intrinsic to the volume and usually participate in an overarching design of the book. Kunigunde's book, for example, contains five tracts on the Passion, three of which make up the body of the manuscript. The items are framed by dedicatory materials in praise of the book's patron, whose image is found on the first opening.[88] The first three texts are heavily illustrated, their imagery tying the theme of Christ as knight—prevalent in the first text, *De strenuo milite*—to the *arma Christi*, including the side wound.[89] The capacity for transness as virtue in this monastic context is introduced by the author of the texts, who, in his dedication to Kunigunde, instructs her, "Vos ergo, que femineo pectori virilem inserendo animum in hac pugna cottidie viriliter confligitis, ad arma passionis dominice prudenti usa consilio convolatis. (You, who contend manfully in this battle daily by implanting a male mind in a female breast, hasten to the arms of the Lord's Passion with a plan for their prudent use.)"[90] A further illustration presents the trans-capable Kunigunde as a model of devotion to the side wound. Kunigunde, in the same habit as she wears in the presentation image, is shown kneeling in prayer before Christ, now descended from the cross and with his side wound on show. Her eyes are directed towards the wound, and his rubricated command reads, "aspice vuln*era* sevaq*ue* verbera que toleravi (Look at the wounds and savage blows that I have endured.)"[91] Here, the situation of the wound image within the book opens up the monastic space for trans iconographic connection.

Later images are often found in lay books of hours, in sections adapted to the wishes of their patrons. Sometimes these images were added on individual leaves, either commissioned for the construction of the book,

87 Easton, "Wound of Christ," 395–97.

88 Rudy, "Touching the Book," 247–48.

89 Toussaint, *Passional der Kunigunde von Böhmen*, 105–41.

90 Toussaint, *Passional der Kunigunde von Böhmen*, 190; see Prague, NK, MS XIV.A.17, fol. 2r.

91 Prague, NK, MS XIV.A.17, fol. 7v. My thanks go to C. E. M. Henderson, Jessica J. Lockhart, and Stephanie J. Lahey for help interpreting this inscription.

or tipped in after the book was made. The eighteen full-page miniatures by the Masters of the Delft Grisailles in the Loftie Hours, for example, all appear on singletons opposite the opening of the prayer they are intended to illustrate.[92] The parchment appears to be of a different quality to that of the written pages, and it is quite likely that these miniatures were commissioned together to illustrate the prayerbook from a separate producer than the rest of the manuscript. Meanwhile, the image of the wound in the Lewkenor Hours is on a cut down square of parchment, tacked to the page with two small stitches in each of the corners.[93] This piece was clearly added after the book was bound, perhaps to fill a blank space or replace another less-satisfactory item. Rudy has termed these kinds of tipped or stitched in images "postcards." Such images were "personal, portable, and capable of being owned by people at a variety of social levels." Rudy demonstrates that, though most examples now survive in manuscripts (due to the increased stability supplied by a binding), paintings on parchment were "demotic," "did not just belong in private manuscripts," and might be made by "amateur artists," as well as by professionals like the Masters of the Delft Grisailles.[94] Such images, through the constellation of their iconography, provided a lay audience with access to the queer and trans potentials set up by images like Kunigunde's.

In the fifteenth century, woodcut images of the wound circulated as indulgences.[95] Ephemeral printed images like this one might be preserved by sticking them into prayerbooks and other volumes or used for a time before they were lost or discarded. The availability of the wound image in a variety of forms, more or less personalized to the user, meant that people could opt in to the generic network they established. It was possible, at any time, to adapt the normative prayerbook towards gender transcendent devotional modes.

92 WAM, MS W.165, fols. 13v, 20v, 23v, 26v, 29v, 32v, 79v, 100v, 107v, 110v (wounds image), 113v, 116v, 118v, 120v, 123v, 125v, 127v, 130v.

93 LPL, MS 545, fol. 78v.

94 Rudy, *Postcards on Parchment*, 313.

95 Olsen, "Penetrating the Void," 325.

CODA

PALEOGRAPHY AND MANUSCRIPT studies are profoundly imaginative disciplines. In order to make connections between the vicissitudes of manuscript transmission and survival and the real lived experience of scribes, readers, and users, scholars have to think creatively through the material record. To some extent, such connections require us to dispense with our own material-textual realities and put ourselves into the mindset of the medieval scribe. Working back through the peculiar and the odd, or even the "usual" and normalized, in the manuscript record requires a stepping back through and layering up of the material interactions a book has had across its lifetime. Such manoeuvres take imagination.

For the study of minoritized histories, imaginative approaches are not just a useful analytical tool, but an indispensable method for producing just and non-violent/violating narratives about the past. In my introduction, I quoted Saidiya Hartman, who formulates *critical fabulation* as a mode of "advancing a series of speculative arguments and exploiting the capacities of the subjunctive (a grammatical mood that expresses doubts, wishes, and possibilities), in fashioning a narrative, which is based upon archival research, and by that I mean a critical reading of the archive that mimes the figurative dimensions of history...to tell an impossible story and to amplify the impossibility of its telling." The structures and strictures of the archive—understood in the Derridean sense of both the physical space of the collection and the items bounded together within that space—have required scholars like Hartman to find ways of seeing truth through absence and creating wholeness out of the fragmentary. Critical fabulation "strain[s] against the limits of the archive to write a cultural history of the captive, and, at the same time, enact[s] the impossibility of representing the lives of the captives precisely through the process of narration."[1] Trans archives, and the methods we have been taught to parse them, are similarly fragmented. By offering a subjunctive past ("if it were"), we open imaginative possibilities for the present future.

1 Hartman, "Venus in Two Acts," 11.

The interventions in this book have asked readers to set aside some conventional approaches to manuscript studies method in favour of imagining something other. In fact, we might contend that imagining something other is just what trans people *do*. Realizing that one is trans requires a person to step outside of what they have been told—by friends, family, and/or society—and ask, how might things be different? How could they be better? And while the world might not always be there to help, things can be better. Trans affirming healthcare has some of the highest satisfaction rates of any medical interventive.[2] Permanent desistance rates after hormone therapy rank as low as 4 percent.[3] But even without considering affirmative medical intervention (which is not sought by all trans and gender non-conforming people), Karen Barad contends that by understanding our embodiment as a series of interactions with the world around us, we enter into a perpetual state of re-becoming: "Not imaginaries of some future or elsewhere to arrive at or be achieved as a political goal but, rather, imaginaries with material existences in the thick now of the present."[4] We have cultivated present futures by imagining that change is possible.

This book asks manuscript scholars to reorient their imaginative skills "to imagine what liberatory archival practice may look like."[5] I have suggested some possibilities—tactics—in medieval manuscript studies for navigating the white supremacist cisheteropatriarchal structures that marked the field's formation, the legacies of which perpetuate in modern methodologies. Some have been more successful than others: they were experiments, after all! And not all will appeal to every reader. Our experiences like those of our historical counterparts, are culturally contingent and socially embedded. However, these approaches, I suggest, offer avenues to strengthen,

2 James, Herman, and Heng-Lehtinen, *Early Insights*, 17, reports that 94 percent of those who had received gender affirming care reported an improvement in their well being and quality of life. Bustos, Bustos, Mascaro, Del Corral, Forte, Ciudad, Kim, Langstein, and Manrique, "Regret after Gender-Affirmation Surgery" reports that the regret rates after gender affirming surgery are less than 1 percent. An erratum was published in the same journal in 2022 in which "The systematic review was re-conducted, and the meta-analysis was re-run with the updated numbers with no significant or major changes." By comparison, regret rates after total knee arthroplasty (knee replacement surgery), for example, range between 6 and 30 percent. See Mahdi, Svantesson, Wretenberg, and Hälleberg-Nyman, "Patients' Experiences."

3 See Feigerlova, "Prevalence of Detransition."

4 Barad, "Transmaterialities," 388.

5 Caswell, *Urgent Archives*, 12.

deeper, and diversify the field. By combining book historical imaginations with trans imaginaries, we open space for other approaches, turning the field toward liberatory justice. I turn the three tactics I developed toward locating historic trans experience and harnessing it as trans historic community building and care work. As I suggested at the start of this book: when facing down the destruction of trans literature and learning in the digital sphere, relearning methods for cultivating, maintaining, and tending trans community through the material text will be crucial to our survival. The need for sustenance and nourishment is acute. But others may benefit from such methods too. In a moment when AI is degrading (and surveilling) digital communications in the service of technofascism, revitalizing the messy material connections offered by the book-object can serve as a lifeline—a line of flight into what is real and felt.

The experiments undertaken here offer a glimpse of a present future for manuscript studies. Other areas of bibliography require similar attention. Print bibliography operates through paradigms that overlap with those of manuscript studies in some places and diverge in others. For instance, the shared embodied language of letterforms (tail, shoulder, ear, neck) is uniquely gendered in the casting of type. Here, male and female blocks (the catches on the upper and lower half of the type matrix) are pressed together, holding the mold in place to produce a piece of type: "their mechanistic heterosexual coupling is an essential part of the creation of words."[6] The language is reflective of compulsory cisheterosexuality in the age of mechanical reproduction. But I am not carving out a field alone: trans bibliography is here, and it s growing. The queer bibliography conferences, and the publications derived from them, have showcased work on materials from the seventeenth-century handpress to twentieth-century ephemera. Kadin Henningsen, Liz Ott, and Brandi Adams have, in various presentations, issued methodological challenges to combat the ontological assumptions of the field.[7] Carlisle Yingst analyzes Romantic-era pseudonymous writers (like David Lyndsay/Mary Diana Dods/Walter Sholto Douglas) through a trans lens, using trans naming practices to trouble bibliographic categories of authenticity and forgery.[8] Sonja Drimmer assesses the seductive, yet troubling, status of the trans body in hand-copied woodcut images, upsetting

6 Maruca, "Bodies of Type," 328.

7 Henningsen and Ott, "Bibliography's Trans* Becoming"; and Adams and Henningsen, "Towards a Trans* Bibliography."

8 See Yingst, "Transition by the Book."

progressivist arguments surrounding the uptake of technologies.[9] Heidi Craig, Laura Estill, and Kris L. May make the case for trans-inclusive practices in enumerative bibliography, rather than "aspir[ing] to stability" in publication history, they apply trans-inclusive citational practices to affirm scholars and "challenge[...] binary systems and templates."[10] Across periods, trans bibliographic study remains committed to exposing the cisheterosexist assumptions behind methodological commonplaces and appealing to trans approaches as a tactic to circumvent the cruxes caused by such assumptions.

Like me, these scholars have benefitted most from the more developed fields of trans and queer librarianship. In 2009, K. J. Rawson put out a call for librarians and archivists to consider "environmental accessibility and geosemiotics" as they work with trans collections and trans users.[11] As I did in my final chapter, Rawson emphasizes the importance of touch in activating affective relations with trans objects. Trans archivists and librarians have thought carefully about the places and spaces in which books, documents, and archival objects are kept and how those materials might be accessed. In doing so, they have reiterated that trans and queer bibliographic space is political; that the objects we care for (and those that we exclude), the ways that we talk about them, and the strategies we have for engagement are enmeshed within political and politicized structures. These factors impact whose stories we tell and how we tell them. I am immensely grateful to the book-workers within institutional and grassroots collections for setting the agenda for trans bibliography to follow.

I have been lucky to find connection with trans and queer book-workers and bibliographers, in person and in print. As the need for sustenance and nourishment among members of the trans community becomes more acute, I hope that the approaches laid out here may meet you with connection: connection to a community of trans and queer book historians in the present, but also connection to a trans temporal community of care through the shared intimacies of our constellated pasts. We are here, but we were also there: our books tell us so.

9 Drimmer, "Queer Transmissions."

10 Craig, Estill, and May, "Trans-Inclusive Bibliography," 10 and 9.

11 Rawson, "Desiring Queer(er?) Archival Logics," 129.

BIBLIOGRAPHY

Manuscripts and Archival Documents

Baltimore, Walters Art Museum, MS W.165.

Brighton, East Sussex and Brighton and Hove Record Office, The Keep, Electoral Registers, 1705–1963, East Sussex, England, Eastbourne, P.D.M, Parish of Alciston.

——, East Sussex and Brighton and Hove Records Office, AMS6516/7.

Kew (London), The National Archives, Census of England and Wales, 1911, London, Marylebone, Schedule 354: image, "Census and Voter Lists." *Ancestry.com*. https://www.ancestry.com, accessed June 20, 2024.

——, The National Archives, Census of England and Wales, 1911, London, Marylebone, Schedule 354: image, *Findmypast*. https://www.findmypast.com, accessed June 19, 2024.

——, The National Archives, Royal Hospital Chelsea, Compassionate Allowances, Royal Bounty and Relief Fund, WO 23/116, no. 42, paper no. 70918/9.

London, British Library, MS Additional 37049.

——, British Library, Harley Roll T 11.

——, British Library, MS Royal 14.B.vi.

——, City of Westminster Archives Centre, Electoral Registers 1902–1970, Westminster, London, England, P.D.E. No. 4, Dorset Square and Regent's Park Ward, Div. 1.

——, Lambeth Palace Library, MS 545.

——, The London Archives (formerly Corporation of London Records Office), Plea and Memoranda Roll A34.

——, Senate House Library, MS S.L. V.88.

New Haven, Yale University, Beinecke Library, MS Marston 242.

Oxford, Bodleian Library, MS Auct. D.4.4.

——, Bodleian Library, MS Junius 1.

Paris, Archives nationales de France, P 1403, nos. 38–39.

——, Bibliothèque nationale de France, MS anglais 39.

——, Bibliothèque nationale de France, MS français 547.

Prague, National Library of the Czech Republic, MS XIV.A.17.

San Marino, Huntington Library, MS HM 114.

Vienna, National Library of Austria, MS Cod. 2554.

Washington DC, National Archives, US Department of Labor, Arriving Passenger and Crew Lists, 1820–1957, List or Manifest of Alien Passengers for the United States, S.S. Carmania, Passengers Sailing from Southampton, December 17, 1921, List 4: image, "New York, U.S. Arriving Passenger and Crew Lists." *Ancestry.com*. https://www.ancestry.com, accessed June 20, 2024.

Printed Primary Sources

An Act Relating to Education. FL H1069, 2023 Regular Session. Chapter no. 2023–105.

An Act Relating to Children and Students. IA SF496, 90th General Assembly. Chapter no. 91.

Aelred of Rievaulx. *Treatises and the Pastoral Prayer*. Translated by Theodore Berkeley, Mary Paul Macpherson, and R. Penelope Lawson. Cistercian, 1971.

Bury, Richard de. *Philobiblon*. Translated by Ernest Chester Thomas. Chatto, 1909.

Elstob, Elizabeth. *An English-Saxon Homily on the Birth-Day of St. Gregory Anciently Used in the English-Saxon Church*. Bowyer, 1709.

For Women Scotland Ltd v. The Scottish Ministers. UKSC, case 16 (2025).

Furnivall, F. J., and Alfred W. Pollard, eds. *The Macro Plays*. EETS, e.s. 91. Oxford University Press, 1904. Reprint, 1924.

Gatterer, Johann Christoph. *Elementa artis diplomaticae universalis*. 1798.

Hall, Radclyffe. *The Well of Loneliness*. Cape, 1928. Reprint, 1982.

Heine, Henrich. "Almansor: Eine Tragödie." In *Heine's Werke in Fünfzehn Teilen*. Edited by Erwin Kalischer and Raimund Pissin. Vol. 5. Bong, ca. 1908.

James of Milan, *Stimulus amoris fr. Jacobi Mediolanensis*. Edited by the Priest of the College of St. Bonaventure. Quaracchi, 1905.

Julian of Norwich. *The Shewings of Julian of Norwich*, Part 3. Edited by Georgia Ronan Crampton. Medieval Institute, 1994.

Madden, Fredric, ed. *The Ancient English Romance of Havelok the Dane*. Nicol, Shakspeare, 1828.

——. *The Old English Versions of the Gesta Romanorum*. Nicol, Shakspeare, 1838.

——, and Josiah Forshall, eds. *The Holy Bible, Containing the Old and New Testaments with the Apocryphal Books, in the Early English Versions Made from the Latin Vulgate by John Wycliffe and his Followers*. 4 vols. Oxford University Press, 1850.

Mechthild of Magdeburg. *The Flowing Light of the Godhead*. Translated by Frank Tobin. Paulist, 1998.

Ritson, Joseph, ed. *Ancient Engleish Metrical Romanceës*. Vol. 1. Bulmer, 1802.

Secondary Works

Adams, Brandi K., and Kadin Henningsen. "Towards a Trans* Bibliography of Early Modern English Drama: A Provocation." Trans Bibliography: A Symposium. In person presentation. Harvard University, March 13, 2025.

Adler, Melissa. "'Let's not Homosexualize in the Library Stacks': Liberating Gays in the Library Catalogue." *Journal of the History of Sexuality* 24, no. 3 (2015): 478–507.

Adolpho, Keahi Ka'iwalani, et al. Homosaurus: An International Linked Data Vocabulary. https://homosaurus.org, accessed February 2, 2024.

Agorsah, E. Kofi. "Restitution of Cultural Material to Africa." *Africa Spectrum* 12, no. 3 (1977): 305–8.

Ahmed, Sara. *The Cultural Politics of Emotion*. 2nd ed. Edinburgh University Press, 2014.

——. *Queer Phenomenology: Orientations, Objects, Others*. Duke University Press, 2006.

——, and Jackie Stacey. "Introduction: Dermographies." In *Thinking Through the Skin*. Edited by Sara Ahmed and Jackie Stacey, 1–17. Routledge, 2001.

Allen, Jafari S. "Black/Queer Rhizomatics: Train Up the Child in the Way Ze Should Grow." In *No Tea, No Shade: New Writings in Black Queer Studies*. Edited by E. Patrick Johnson, 27–47. Duke University Press, 2016.

Allen-Goss, Lucy, writing as Jeanne de Montbaston. "Technologies of Touch and Queer Errors." Reading Medieval Books, September 14, 2016. https://readingmedievalbooks.wordpress.com/2016/09/14/technologies-of-touch-and-queer-errors/, accessed July 14, 2025.

Amsler, Mark. "Affective Literacies: Gestures of Reading in the Later Middle Ages." *Essays in Medieval Studies* 18 (2001): 83–110.

Andrews, Tarren, and Tiffany Beechy, eds. "Indigenous Futures and Medieval Pasts." Special issue of *English Language Notes* 58, no. 2 (2020).

Anon. "2025 anti-trans bills tracker." Trans Legislation Tracker. https://translegislation.com/, accessed May 23, 2025.

Anzieu, Didier. *The Skin-Ego*. Translated by Naomi Segal. Routledge, 2016.

Ardizzone, Heidi. *An Illuminated Life: Belle da Costa Greene's Journey from Prejudice to Privilege*. Norton, 2007.

Aris, Rutherford. "Jean Mabillon (1632–1707)." In *Medieval Scholarship: Biographical Studies on the Formation of a Discipline, Volume 1: History*. Edited by Helen Damico and Joseph B. Zavadil, 15–32. Garland, 1995.

Ashe, Laura. "The Originality of the *Orrmulum*." *Early Middle English* 1, no. 1, (2019): 35–54.

Ashley, Florence. "'Trans' is my Gender Modality." In *Trans Bodies, Trans Selves*. Edited by Laura Erickson-Schroth, 22. 2nd ed. Oxford University Press, 2022.

——, Shari Brightly-Brown, and G. Nic Rider. "Beyond the Trans/Cis Binary." *Nature* 630 (June 2024): 293–95.

Baker, Eleanor. "References to Material Texts in Late Medieval English Religious Literature." PhD diss., University of Oxford, 2021.

Barad, Karen. "Transmaterialities: Trans*/Matter/Realities and Queer Political Imaginings." *GLQ: A Journal of Lesbian and Gay Studies* 21, nos. 2–3 (2015): 387–422.

Bart, Patricia R. "Intellect, Influence and Evidence: The Elusive Allure of the Ht Scribe." In *Yee? Baw for Bokes: Essays on Medieval Manuscripts and Poetics in Honor of Hoyt N. Duggan*. Edited by Michael A. Calabrese and Stephen H. A. Shepherd, 219–34. Marymount Institute, 2013.

Bauer, Heike. "Burning Sexual Subjects: Books, Homophobia and the Nazi Destruction of the Institute of Sexual Science in Berlin." In *Book Destruction from the Medieval to the Contemporary*. Edited by Gill Partington and Adam Smyth, 17–33. Palgrave, 2014.

——. *The Hirschfeld Archives: Violence, Death, and Modern Queer Culture*. Temple University Press, 2017.

Betancourt, Roland. *Byzantine Intersectionality: Sexuality, Gender, and Race in the Middle Ages*. Princeton University Press, 2020.

——. "Trans In/visibility in Byzantium: Resistance, Resilience, Refusal." Trans Sainthood in Translation, ca. 400–1500. Plenary lecture at German Historical Institute London, May 23, 2025.

Bhinder, Jasmine, and Prashant Uphadhyaya, "Brief History of Gender Affirmation Medicine and Surgery." In *Urological Care for the Transgender Patient: A Comprehensive Guide*. Edited by Dmitriy Nikolavsky and Stephen A. Blakely, 249–54. Springer, 2021.

Bibliographical Society of America. "What is Bibliography?" https://bibsocamer.org/about/what-is-bibliography, accessed October 14, 2024.

Bindman, David. *"Race is Everything": Art and Human Difference*. Reaktion, 2023.

Bischoff, F. M. *Urkundenformate im Mittelalter: Größe, Format und Proportionen von Papsturkunden in Zeiten expandierender Schriftlichkeit: 11.–13. Jahrhundert*. Institut für Historische Hilfswiss, 1996.

Bordalejo, Barbara. "The Genealogy of Texts: Manuscript Traditions and Textual Traditions." *Digital Scholarship in the Humanities* 31, no. 3 (2016): 563–77.

——. "New Stemmatics." *Textual Scholarship*, June 8, 2007. http://www.textualscholarship.org/newstemmatics/index.html, accessed July 14, 2025.

Borrie, Michael. "Thompson, Sir Edward Maunde (1840–1929)." In *Oxford Dictionary of National Biography*. Oxford University Press, 2010. https://www.oxforddnb.com/display/10.1093/ref:odnb/9780198614128.001.0001/odnb-9780198614128-e-36488, accessed July 14, 2025.

Boyd, David Lorenzo, and Ruth Mazo Karras. "The Interrogation of a Male Transvestite Prostitute in Fourteenth-Century London." *GLQ: A Journal of Lesbian and Gay Studies* 1 (1995): 479–85.

——. "*Ut cum muliere*: A Male Transvestite Prostitute in Fourteenth Century London." In *Premodern Sexualities*. Edited by Louise Fradenburg and Carla Freccero, 99–116. Routledge, 1996.

Braidotti, Rosi. "Teratologies." In *Deleuze and Feminist Theory*. Edited by I. Buchanan and C. Colebrook, 156–72. Edinburgh University Press, 2000.

Bustos, V. P., et al. "Regret after Gender-Affirmation Surgery: A Systematic Review and Meta-analysis of Prevalence." *Plastic Reconstructive Surgery Global Open* 9, no. 3 (2021): e3477.

Butler, Judith. *Bodies that Matter: On the Discursive Limits of "Sex."* Routledge, 1993.

——. *Excitable Speech: A Politics of the Performative*. Routledge, 1997.

——. *Gender Trouble: Feminism and the Subversion of Identity*. Routledge, 1990.

——. *Undoing Gender*. Routledge, 2004.

Bychowski, M. W. "Trans Textuality: Dysphoria in the Depths of Medieval Skin." *postmedieval* 9 (2018): 318–33.

——. "The Transgender Turn: Eleanor Rykener Speaks Back." In *Trans Historical: Gender Plurality Before the Modern*. Edited by Greta LaFleur, Masha Raskolnikov, and Anna Kłosowska, 95–113. Cornell University Press, 2021.

Bynum, Caroline Walker. *Jesus as Mother: Studies in the Spirituality of the High Middle Ages*. University of California Press, 1982.

——. "Violent Imagery in Late Medieval Piety." *German Historical Institute Bulletin* 30 (2002): 3–36.

Calhoun, Joshua. *The Nature of the Page: Poetry, Papermaking, and the Ecology of Texts in Renaissance England*. University of Pennsylvania Press, 2020.

Camille, Michael. "The Book as Flesh and Fetish in Richard de Bury's *Philobiblon*." In *The Body and the Book*. Edited by Dolores Warwick Frese and Katherine O'Brien O'Keeffe, 34–77. University of Notre Dame Press, 1997.

Cannon, Loren. *The Politicization of Trans Identity: An Analysis of Backlash, Scapegoating, and Dog-Whistling from Obergefell to Bostock*. Lexington, 2022.

Carter, Julian. "Embracing Transition, or Dancing in the Folds of Time." In *The Transgender Studies Reader 2*. Edited by Susan Stryker and Aren Z. Aizura, 130–43. Routledge, 2013.

Caswell, Michelle. *Urgent Archives: Enacting Liberatory Memory Work*. Routledge, 2021.

Cataldi, Sue L. *Emotion, Depth, and Flesh: A Study of Sensitive Space*. State University of New York Press, 1993.

Center on Reproductive Health, Law, and Policy. "Shield Laws for Reproductive and Gender Affirming Health Care: A State Law Guide." UCLA Law, September 2024. https://williamsinstitute.law.ucla.edu/publications/shield-laws-fact-sheets/, accessed July 15, 2025.

Cerquiglini, Bernard. *Éloge de la variante: Histoire critique de la philologie*. Seuil, 1989.

——. *In Praise of the Variant: A Critical History of Philology*. Translated by Betsy Wing. Johns Hopkins University Press, 1999.

Charmaille, François·e. "Trans Climates of the European Middle Ages, 500–1300." *Speculum* 98, no. 3 (2023): 673–1018.

Chess, Simone. *Male-to-Female Crossdressing in Early Modern English Literature: Gender, Performance, and Queer Relations*. Routledge, 2016.

Chess, Simone, Colby Gordon, and Will Fisher, eds. "Early Modern Trans Studies." Special issue of *Journal for Early Modern Cultural Studies* 19, no. 4 (2019).

Chu, Andrea Long, and Emmett Harsin Drager. "After Trans Studies." *TSQ: Transgender Studies Quarterly* 6, no. 1 (2019): 103–16.

Ciallela, Erica, and Philip S. Palmer, eds. *Belle da Costa Greene: A Librarians Legacy*. Morgan Library, 2024.

Cifor, Marika. "Presence, Absence, and Victoria's Hair: Examining Affect and Embodiment in Trans Archives." *TSQ: Transgender Studies Quarterly* 2, no. 4 (2015): 645–49.

Clancy, Kate, Agustin Fuentes, Caroline M. VanSickle, and Catherine Clune-Taylor. "Biology Is Not Binary." *American Scientist* 112, no. 2 (2024): 78–81.

Clanchy, Michael. *From Memory to the Written Record: England 1066–1307*. 3rd ed. Wiley-Blackwell, 2013.

Clemens, Raymond, and Timothy Graham. *Introduction to Manuscript Studies*. Cornell University Press, 2007.

Coleman, Joyce. *Public Reading and the Reading Public in Late Medieval England and France*. Cambridge University Press, 1996.

Collins, Patricia Hill. *Black Feminist Thought: Knowledge, Consciousness, and the Politics of Empowerment*. 2nd ed. Routledge, 2000.

Coman, Jonah. "Queering Christ: Habitus Theology as Trans-Embodied Incarnation in Late Medieval Culture." PhD diss., Glasgow School of Art, 2019.

Coulthard, Glen Sean. *Red Skin, White Masks: Rejecting the Colonial Politics of Recognition*. University of Minnesota Press, 2014.

Cowdery, Taylor. "Apprentice Work in the Age of Chaucer: Eleanor Rykener and Perkin Revelour." *The Biannual Congress of the New Chaucer Society*. In person presentation, Westin Pasadena, July 18, 2024.

Craig, Heidi, Laura Estill, and Kris L. May. "A Rationale for Trans-Inclusive Bibliography." *Textual Cultures* 16, no. 2 (2023): 1–28.

Crane, Susan. "Duxworth Redux: The Paris Manuscript of the *Canterbury Tales*." In *Manuscript, Narrative, Lexicon: Essays on Literary and Cultural Transmission in Honor of Whitney F. Bolton*. Edited by Robert Boenig and Kathleen Davis, 17–44. Bucknell University Press, 2000.

Crow, Martin M. "John of Angoulême and his Chaucer Manuscript." *Speculum* 17 (1942): 86–99.

——. "*The Reeves Tale* in the Hands of a North Midland Scribe." *Studies in English* 18 (1938): 14–24.

Da Rold, Orietta. *Paper in Medieval England: From Pulp to Fictions*. Cambridge University Press, 2020.

Darnton, Robert. "What is the History of Books?" *Daedalus* 111, no. 3 (1982): 65–83.

Davis, Bob. "Using Archives to Identify the Trans* Women of Casa Susanna." *TSQ: Transgender Studies Quarterly* 2, no. 4 (2015): 621–34.

Delany, Sheila. "Medieval Marxists: A Tradition." *Medieval Feminist Forum: A Journal of Gender and Sexuality* 30 (2001): 9–15.

Deleuze, Gilles, and Félix Guattari. *A Thousand Plateaus: Capitalism and Schizophrenia*. Translated by Brian Massumi. University of Minnesota Press, 1987.

DeVun, Leah. *The Shape of Sex: Nonbinary Gender from Genesis to the Renaissance*. Columbia University Press, 2021.

Dinshaw, Carolyn. *Getting Medieval: Sexualities and Communities, Pre- and Postmodern*. Duke University Press, 1999.

Drimmer, Sonja. "Connoisseurship, Art History, and the Paleographical Impasse." *Speculum* 97, no. 2 (2022): 415–68.

——. "Queer Transmissions: English Manuscript, Italian Print and a Discomforting History of the Book." *Renaissance Studies* 39, no. 4 [preprint] (2025): 1–26.

duCille, Ann. "On Canons: Anxious History and the Rise of Black Feminist Literary Studies." In *The Cambridge Companion to Feminist Literary Theory*. Edited by Ellen Rooney, 29–52. Cambridge University Press, 2006.

Dunbar, Anthony W. "Introducing Critical Race Theory to Archival Studies: Getting the Conversation Started." *Archival Science* 6, no. 1 (2006): 109–29.

Duranti, Luciana. *Diplomatics: New Uses for an Old Science*. Scarecrow, 1998.

Durling, Nancy Vine. "British Library MS Harley 2253: A New Reading of the Passion Lyrics in Their Manuscript Context." *Viator* 40, no. 1 (2009): 271–307.

Easton, Martha. "The Wound of Christ, the Mouth of Hell: Appropriations and Inversions of Female Anatomy in the Middle Ages." In *The Making and Meaning of Illuminated Medieval Manuscripts, Art and Architecture: Tributes to J. J. Alexander*. Edited by Susan L'Engle and Gerald B. Guest, 395–414. Miller, 2006.

Edwards, A. S. G. "Eleanor Prescott Hammond (1866–1933): Pioneer Scholar of Middle English Manuscript Study." In *Women Medievalists and the Academy*. Edited by Jane Chance, 91–98. University of Wisconsin Press, 2005.

——. "What is Palaeography For?" *The Mediæval Journal* 8, no. 2 (2018): 21–40.

Ellis, Havelock. "The Sterilization of the Unfit." *The Eugenics Review* 1, no. 3 (1909): 203–6.

——, and John Addington Symonds. *Sexual Inversion*. 2 vols. Wilson, 1897.

Equality and Human Rights Commission. "An Interim Update on the Practical Implications of the UK Supreme Court Judgment," April 25, 2025. https://www.equalityhumanrights.com/media-centre/interim-update-practical-implications-uk-supreme-court-judgment, accessed July 15, 2025.

Eze, Anne-Marie. "The Ballad of Belle da Costa Greene: Librarian as Medievalist." In *Belle da Costa Greene: A Librarian's Legacy*. Edited by Erica Ciallela and Philip S. Palmer, 133–70. Morgan Museum, 2024.

Feigerlova, Eva. "Prevalence of Detransition in Persons Seeking Gender-Affirming Hormonal Treatments: A Systematic Review." *Journal of Sexual Medicine* 22, no. 2 (January 9, 2025). https://www.doi.org/10.1093/jsxmed/qdae186.

Ferguson, Susan. *Women and Work: Feminism, Labour, and Social Reproduction*. Pluto, 2020.

Fishburn, Matthew. "Books are Weapons: Wartime Responses to the Nazi Book Fires of 1933." *Book History* 10 (2007): 223–51.

——. *Burning Books*. Palgrave, 2008.

Fisher, Matthew. *Scribal Authorship and the Writing of History in Medieval England*. Ohio State University Press, 2012.

Fister, Barbara. "Trumping Ownership with Open Access: A Manifesto." *Library Journal* (April 1, 2010). Reprinted as "Liberation Bibliography." https://barbarafister.net/cv/liberation-bibliography/, accessed September 10, 2024.

Fitzgerald, Tanya. "Academic Networks, Professional Connections, and Social Circles: Reading the Scholarly Life of Caroline Spurgeon." *Annali di Storia della Università italiana* 26, no. 2 (2022): 9–21.

Foner, Daria Rose. "The Education of Belle da Costa Greene." In *Belle da Costa Greene: A Librarians Legacy*. Edited by Erica Ciallela and Philip S. Palmer, 45–67. Morgan Museum, 2024.

Forrest, Kathleen V. *Lesbian Pulp Fiction: The Sexually Intrepid World of Lesbian Paperback Novels 1950–1965*. Cleis, 2005.

Freeman, Edward A. *The Reign of William Rufus and the Ascension of Henry the First*. Vol. 1. Clarendon, 1882.

Freeman, Elizabeth. "Time Binds, or, Erotohistory." *Social Text* 84–85, nos. 3–4 (2005): 57–68.

——. *Time Binds: Queer Temporalities, Queer Histories*. Duke University Press, 2010.

Garnett, R. "The Late Sir Edward A. Bond, K. C. B." *The Library* s1-x, no. 1 (1898): 112–14.

Gennari-Santori, Flaminia. "'This Feminine Scholar': Belle da Costa Greene and the Shaping of J. P. Morgan's Legacy." *Visual Resources* 33, nos. 1–2 (2017): 182–97.

Ghosh, Amitav. "The Slave of MS. H.6." In *Subaltern Studies VII: Writings on South Asian History and Society*. Edited by Partha Chatterjee and Gyanendra Pandey, 159–220. Oxford University Press, 1992.

Gierl, Martin. *Geschichte als präzisierte Wissenschaft: Johann Christoph Gatterer und die Historiographie des 18. Jahrhunderts im ganzen Umfang*. Frommann Holzboog, 2012.

Gillespie, Diane F. "Virginia Woolf and the War on Books: Cultural Heritage and Dis-Heritage in the 1930s." In *Virginia Woolf and Heritage*. Edited by Jane de Gay, Tom Breckin, and Anna Reus, 176–82. Clemson University Press, 2017.

Gill-Peterson, Jules. *Histories of the Transgender Child*. University of Minnesota Press, 2018.

Gould, Stephen Jay. *The Mismeasure of Man*. Norton, 1981.

Greenspan, Ezra, and Jonathan Rose. "An Introduction to Book History." *Book History* 1 (1998): ix–xi.

Greetham, David. "Phylum–Tree–Rhizome." *Huntington Library Quarterly* 58, no. 1 (1995): 99–126.

Greir, James. "Lachmann, Bédier, and the Bipartite Stemma: Towards a Responsible Application of the Common-Error Method." *Revue d'histoire des textes* 18 (1989): 263–78.

Gretsch, Mechthild. "Elizabeth Elstob: A Scholar's Fight for Anglo-Saxon Studies. Part 1." *Anglia* 117, no. 2 (1999): 163–200.

——. "Elizabeth Elstob: A Scholar's Fight for Anglo-Saxon Studies. Part 2." *Anglia* 117, no. 4 (1999): 481–524.

Grigely, Joseph. *Textualterity: Art, Theory, and Textual Criticism*. University of Michigan Press, 1995.

Gumbert, J. P. "Skins, Sheets, and Quires." In *New Directions in Later Medieval Manuscript Studies*. Edited by Derek Pearsall, 81–90. Boydell, 2000.

Gundu, Zacharys. "Looted Nigerian Heritage: An Interrogatory Discourse around Repatriation." *Contemporary Journal of African Studies* 7, no. 1 (2020): 47–66.

Haas, Renate. "Caroline F. E. Spurgeon (1869–1942): First Woman Professor of English in England." In *Women Medievalists and the Academy*. Edited by Jane Chance, 99–109. University of Wisconsin Press, 2005.

Halberstam, Jack. *In a Queer Time and Place: Transgender Bodies, Subcultural Lives*. New York University Press, 2005.

Hammond, Eleanor Prescott. "Ashmole 59 and other Shirley Manuscripts." *Anglia* 30 (1907): 320–48.

——. "A Scribe of Chaucer." *Modern Philology* 27, no. 1 (1929): 27–33.

——. "Two British Museum Manuscripts: (Harley 2251 and Adds. 34360): A Contribution to the Bibliography of John Lydgate." *Anglia* 28 (1905): 1–28.

Hartman, Saidiya. "Venus in Two Acts." *Small Axe* 12, no. 2 (2008): 1–14.

Henningsen, Kadin. "'Calling [Herself] Eleanor': Gender Labor and Becoming a Woman in the Rykener Case." *Medieval Feminist Forum: A Journal of Gender and Sexuality* 55, no. 1 (2019): 249–66.

Henningsen, Kadin, and Liz Ott. "Who's Afraid of the Ideal Copy: Bibliography's Trans* Becoming." *Queer Bibliography*. In person presentation. University of California, Los Angeles, July 26, 2024.

Heyam, Kit. *Before We Were Trans: A New History of Gender*. Basic, 2022.

Hiatt, Alfred. "Diplomatic Arts: Hickes Against Mabillon in the Republic of Letters." *Journal of the History of Ideas* 70, no. 3 (2009): 351–73.

Hicks, Dan. *The Brutish Museums: The Benin Bronzes, Colonial Violence and Cultural Restitution*. Pluto, 2020.

Holsinger, Bruce, "Medieval Studies, Postcolonial Studies, and the Genealogies of Critique." *Speculum* 77, no. 4 (2002): 1195–227.

——. *On Parchment: Animals, Archives, and the Making of Culture from Herodotus to the Digital Age*. Yale University Press, 2023.

Honma, Todd. "Trippin' over the Color Line: The Invisibility of Race in Library and Information Sciences." *InterActions: UCLA Journal of Information and Education Studies* 1, no. 2 (2005). https://doi.org/10.5070/D412000540

Hsu, V. Jo. *Constellating Home: Trans and Queer Asian American Rhetorics*. Ohio State University Press, 2022.

Hughes, Shaun F. D. "Elizabeth Elstob (1683–1756) and the Limits of Women's Agency in Early-Eighteenth-Century England." In *Women Medievalists and the Academy*. Edited by Jane Chance, 3–24. University of Wisconsin Press, 2005.

James, S. E., J. L. Herman, and R. Heng-Lehtinen. *Early Insights: A Report of the 2022 U.S. Transgender Survey*. National Center for Transgender Equality, 2022.

Johnson, Carla K. "Health Info Wiped from Federal Websites Following Trump Order Targetting Transgender Rights." *PBS News*, January 31, 2025. https://www.pbs.org/newshour/health/health-info-wiped-from-federal-websites-following-trump-order-targeting-transgender-rights, accessed July 14, 2025.

Johnson, E. Patrick. "'Quare' Studies, or (Almost) Everything I Know About Queer Studies I Learned from My Grandmother." *Text and Performance Quarterly* 21, no. 1 (2001): 1–25.

Johnston, Andrew James, Wolfram R. Keller, and Henry Ravenhall. "Introduction: Touching Troy." *Anglia* 142, no. 3 (2024): 419–27.

Kabir, Ananya Jahanara. "Analogy in Translation: Imperial Rome, Medieval England and British India." In *Postcolonial Approaches to the European Middle Ages: Translating Cultures*. Edited by Ananya Jahanara Kabir and Deanne Williams, 183–204. Cambridge University Press, 2005.

Kane, George and E. Talbot Donaldson, eds. *Piers Plowman: The B-Version*. Athlone, 1975

Karsten, Bethany. "The Trans Literature Project: A Practical Guide to Resisting Censorship." *The Transfeminine Review*, November 13, 2024. https://thetransfemininereview.com/2024/11/13/a-practical-guide-to-resisting-censorship/, accessed July 15, 2025.

Kay, Sarah. *Animal Skins and the Reading Self in Medieval Latin and French Bestiaries*. University of Chicago Press, 2017.

——. "Original Skin: Flaying, Reading, and Thinking in the Legend of Saint Bartholomew and Other Works." *Journal of Medieval and Early Modern Studies* 36, no. 1 (2006): 35–73.

Kennedy, Kathleen. *Illuminating Media: Transmitting the Renaissance in England, 1450–1500*. Concordia University Press, 2025.

Kiernan, James G. "Responsibility in Sexual Perversion." *Chicago Medical Recorder* 3 (1982): 135–210.

Kim, Dorothy. "Belle da Costa Greene, Book History, Race, and Medieval Studies." *Quimbandas* 1, no. 1 (2020): 43–61.

——, and M. W. Bychowski, eds. "Visions of Medieval Trans Feminism." Special issue of *Medieval Feminist Forum: A Journal of Gender and Sexuality* 55, no. 1 (2019).

Kirsch, Gesa E., and Liz Rohan, eds. *Beyond the Archives: Research as a Lived Process*. Southern Illinois University Press, 2008.

Knuth, Rebecca. *Libricide: The Regime-Sponsored Destruction of Books and Libraries in the Twentieth Century*. Praeger, 2003.

Krafft-Ebing, Richard Freiherr von. *Psychopathia Sexualis: Eine Klinisch-Forensische Studie*. Ferdinand Enke, 1886.

Krygier, John. "Mermaid Series." A Series of Series: 20th-Century Publishers Book Series. Ohio Wesleyan University, 2016. https://seriesofseries.com/mermaid-series/, accessed July 14, 2025.

Laborderie, Olivier de. "The First Manuals of English History: Two Late Thirteenth-Century Genealogical Rolls of the Kings of England in the Royal Collection." *Electronic British Library Journal* art. 4 (2014). https://doi.org/10.23636/1084.

LaFleur, Greta, Masha Raskolnikov, and Anna Kłosowska, eds. *Trans Historical: Gender Plurality before the Modern*. Cornell University Press, 2021.

Lewis, Charleton T., and Charles Short. *A Latin Dictionary Founded on Andrews' Edition of Freund's Latin Dictionary: Revised, Enlarged, and in Great Part Rewritten*. Clarendon, 1879

Lewis, Flora. "The Wound in Christ's Side and the Instruments of Christ's Passion: Gendered Experience and Response." In *Women and the Book: Assessing the Visual Evidence*. Edited by Lesley Smith and Jane H. M. Taylor, 204–28. British Library, 1997.

Livingstone, Jo. "Racism, Medievalism, and the White Supremacists of Charlottesville." *The New Republic*, August 15, 2017. https://newrepublic.com/article/144320/racism-medievalism-white-supremacists-charlottesville, accessed July 14, 2025.

Lochrie, Karma. "Mystical Acts, Queer Tendencies." In *Constructing Medieval Sexuality*. Edited by Karma Lochrie, Peggy McCracken, and James S. Schultz, 180–200. University of Minnesota Press, 1997.

Lomuto, Sierra. "Belle da Costa Greene and the Undoing of 'Medieval' Studies *boundary 2* 50, no. 3 (2023): 1–30.

——, ed. "The 'Medieval' Undone: Imagining a New Global Past." Special issue of *boundary 2* 50, no. 3 (2023).

Love, Heather. *Feeling Backward: Loss and the Politics of Queer History*. Harvard University Press, 2007.

——. "Queer." *TSQ: Transgender Studies Quarterly* 1, nos. 1–2 (2014): 172–76.

Lowe, Lisa. *The Intimacies of Four Continents*. Duke University Press, 2015.

Lynch, Lee. "Cruising the Libraries." In *Lesbian and Gay Studies and the Teaching of English: Postions, Pedagogies, and Cultural Politics*. Edited by William J. Spurling, 3–13. National Council of Teachers, 2000.

Magnani, Roberta, and Diane Watt. "Towards a Queer Philology." *postmedieval* 9 (2018): 252–68.

Magnus-Hirschfeld-Gesellschaft e. V., Forschungsstelle zur Geschichte der Sexualwissenschaft. "Sammlungsschwerpunkte." https://magnus-hirschfeld.de/bibliothek-und-archiv/sammlungsschwerpunkte/, accessed April 16, 2025.

Mahdi, Amir, Mia Svantesson, Per Wretenberg, and Maria Hälleberg-Nyman. "Patients' Experiences of Discontentment One Year After Total Knee Arthroplasty: A Qualitative Study." *BMC Musculoskeletal Disorders* 21, no. 29 (2020). https://doi.org/10.1186/s12891-020-3041-y.

Maillets, Clovis. *Les genre fluids: De Jeanne d'Arc aux saintes trans*. Arkhè, 2020.

Mann, Regis. "Theorizing 'What Could have Been': Black Feminism, Historical Memory, and the Politics of Reclamation." *Women's Studies* 40 (2011): 575–99.

Mara-McKay, Nico, with A. E. Brown, Jonah Coman, Elizabeth Elliott, M. C. Garcia, Hannah Victoria, Kim Zarins, et al. "A Bibliography of Medieval Trans Studies." Working document. May, 2021. https://docs.google.com/document/d/1St09yZA02x6RMl2Do4HcplQt0JnKfN9jUVEn5w15dqA/edit?usp=sharing.

Markowitz, Sally. *The Gender Binary and the Invention of Race*. Routledge, 2024.

Martineau, Jarrett. "Creative Combat: Indigenous Art, Resurgence and Decolonization." PhD diss., University of Victoria, 2015.

Maruca, Lisa. "Bodies of Type: The Work of Textual Production in English Printers' Manuals." *Eighteenth-Century Studies* 36, no. 3 (2003): 321–43.

Maruca, Lisa, and Kate Ozment. "What is Critical Bibliography?" *Criticism* 64, no. 3 (2023): 231–36.

Matthews, David. *The Making of Middle English, 1765–1910*. University of Minnesota Press, 1999.

Mattison, J. R., and Hannah K. Ryley, eds. "Big Data and Manuscript Studies: Some Reflections on a Methodology." Special issue of *Digital Philology* 14, no. 1 (2025).

McAvoy, Liz Herbert. "'The Moders Service': Motherhood as Matrix in Julian of Norwich." *Mystics Quarterly* 24, no. 4 (1998): 181–97.

McCracken, Peggy. *The Skin of the Beast: Sovereignty and Animality in Medieval France*. Chicago University Press, 2017.

Meehan, Kasey, Sabrina Baêta, Tasslyn Magnusson, and Madison Markham. "Banned in the USA: Beyond the Shelves." PEN America, November 1, 2024. https://pen.org/report/beyond-the-shelves/, accessed July 14, 2025.

Menon, Madhavi. *Unhistorical Shakespeare: Queer Theory in Shakespearean Literature and Film*. Palgrave, 2008.

Meyerowitz, Joanne. *How Sex Changed: A History of Transsexuality in the United States*. Harvard University Press, 2002.

Miller, Peter N. *History and its Objects: Antiquarianism and Material Culture since 1500*. Cornell University Press, 2017.

Momma, Haruko. *From Philology to English Studies: Language and Culture in the Nineteenth Century*. Cambridge University Press, 2013.

Mooney, Linne, and Estelle Stubbs. *Scribes in the City: London Guildhall Clerks and the Dissemination of Middle English Literature, 1375–1425*. York Medieval, 2013.

Moreshead, Abigail. "Gender and Para-Academic Labor: The Invisible Translators of Old English and their Legacy in Digital Humanities." *Nineteenth-Century Gender Studies* 18, no. 2 (2022): http://ncgsjournal.com/issue182/moreshead.html, accessed July 14, 2025.

Moretti, Franco. "Style, Inc. Reflections of Seven Thousand Titles (British Novels, 1740–1850)." *Critical Inquiry* 36, no. 1 (2009): 134–58.

Morse, Mary. *English Birth Girdles: Devotions for Women in "Travell of Childe."* Medieval Institute Publications, 2024.

Muñoz, José Esteban. *Cruising Utopia: The Then and There of Queer Futurity*. New York University Press, 2009.

Miyashiro, Adam. "Our Deeper Past: Race, Settler-colonialism, and Medieval Heritage Politics." *Literature Compass* 16, nos. 9–10 (2019): e.12550.

National Institutes of Health. "Understanding Human Genetic Variation." NIH Curriculum Supplement Series. National Library of Medicine. https://www.ncbi.nlm.nih.gov/books/NBK20363, accessed October 5, 2024.

Nelson, Ingrid. *Lyric Tactics: Poetry, Genre, and Practice in Later Medieval England*. University of Pennsylvania Press, 2017.

Nichols, Stephen. "Introduction: Philology in a Manuscript Culture." *Speculum* 65, no. 1 (1990): 1–10.

Nilgen, Ursula. "Amtsgenealogie und Amtsheiligkeit. Königs- und Bischofsreihen in der Kunstpropaganda des Hochmittelalters." In *Studien zur mittelalterlichen Kunst, 800–1250: Festschrift für Florentine Mütherich zum 70. Geburtstag*. Edited by Katharina Bierbrauer, Peter K. Klein, and Willibald Sauerländer, 217–34. Prestel, 1985.

Noble, Malcom and Sarah Pyke. "A Bibliographical Gathering: Reflecting on 'Queer Bibliography: Tools, Methods, Practices, Approaches.'" *The Journal of Electronic Publishing* 28, no. 1 (2025): 245–61.

——. "Queer Bibliography: A Rationale." *PBSA* 18, no. 2 (2024): 147–69.

Noonan, Sarah. "Bodies of Parchment: Representing the Passion and Reading Manuscripts in Late Medieval England." PhD diss., Washington University in St. Louis, 2010.

Noone, Chris, et al. "Critically Appraising the Cass Report: Methodological Flaws and Unsupported Claims." *BMC Medical Research Methodology* 25, no. 128 (2025): 1–18.

Office of the High Commissioner. "UN Experts Warn of Legal Uncertainty and Rights Implications Following UK Supreme Court Ruling." United Nations Human Rights. May 22, 2025. https://www.ohchr.org/en/press-releases/2025/05/un-experts-warn-legal-uncertainty-and-rights-implications-following-uk, accessed July 15, 2025.

Olsen, Vebeke. "Penetrating the Void: Picturing the Wound in Christ's Side as a Performative Space." In *Wounds and Wound Repair in Medieval Culture*. Edited by Larissa Tracy and Kelly DeVries, 313–39. Brill, 2016.

Ozment, Kate. "Rationale for Feminist Bibliography." *Textual Cultures* 13, no. 1 (2020): 149–78.

Panofsky, Aaron, and Joan Donovan. "Genetic Ancestry Testing Among White Nationalists: From Identity Repair to Citizen Science." *Social Studies of Science* 49, no. 5 (2019): 653–81.

Pearce, Ruth. *Understanding Trans Health: Discourse, Power and Possibility*. Bristol University Press, 2022.

Powell, Malea, Daisy Levy, Andrea Riley-Mukavetz, Marilee Brooks-Gillies, Maria Novotny and Jennifer Fisch-Ferguson. "Our Story Begins Here: Constellating Cultural Rhetorics." *enculturation: A Journal of Rhetoric, Writing, and Culture* 18 (October 25, 2014): https://enculturation.net/our-story-begins-here#_edn1, accessed July 14, 2025.

Price, Leah. "Introduction: Reading Matter." *PMLA* 121, no. 1 (2006): 9–16.

Prince, Virginia. "'Breaking the Code' and FPE Membership List." *Transvestia* 19 (1963): 74–75.

Pritchard, Eric Darnell. *Fashioning Lives: Black Queers and the Politics of Literacy*. Southern Illinois University Press, 2016.

Rajendran, Shyama. "Undoing 'the Vernacular': Dismantling Structures of Raciolinguistic Supremacy." *Literature Compass* 16 (2019): e12544.

Rambaran-Olm, Mary, and Erik Wade. "What's in a Name? The Past and Present Racism in 'Anglo-Saxon' Studies." *The Yearbook of English Studies* 52 (2022): 135–53.

——, M. Breann Leake, and Micah Goodrich, eds. "Race, Revulsion, and Revolution." Special issue of *postmedieval* 11, no. 4 (2020).

Ramirez, Mario H. "Being Assumed not to Be: A Critique of Whiteness as an Archival Imperative." *The American Archivist* 78, no. 2 (2015): 339–56.

Ramos, Eduardo. "Philology and Racist Appropriations of the Medieval." *Literature Compass* 20, nos. 7–9 (2023): e.12734.

Rawson, K. J. "Accessing Transgender // Desiring Queer(er?) Archival Logics." *Archivaria* 68 (2009): 123–40.

——, and Charles E. Morris III. "Queer Archives/Archival Queers." In *Theorizing Histories of Rhetoric*. Edited by Michelle Ballif, 74–89. Southern Illinois University Press, 2013.

Reed, Erin. "Protests Erupt at Stonewall After Trump Removes Trans People from Monument Site." *Erin in the Morning*, February 14, 2025. https://www.erininthemorning.com/p/protests-erupt-at-stonewall-after, accessed July 14, 2025.

Rich, Adrienne. "Compulsory Heterosexuality and Lesbian Existence." *Signs* 5, no. 4 (1980): 631–60.

Riley-Mukavetz, Andrea, and Malea Powell. "Making Native Space for Graduate Students: A Story of Indigenous Rhetorical Practice." In *Survivance, Sovereignty, and Story: Teaching American Indian Rhetorics*. Edited by Lisa King, Rose Gubele, and Joyce Rain Anderson, 138–59. Utah State University Press, 2015.

Robertson, Elizabeth. *Early English Devotional Prose and the Female Audience*. University of Tennessee Press, 1990.

——. "Feminism and Medieval Studies: Where Have We Been, Where Are We Now, and Where Are We Going? Or, What Happened to Women in Feminist Studies of the Middle Ages?" In *Founding Feminisms in Medieval Studies: Essays in Honor of E. Jane Burns*. Edited by Laine E. Doggett and Daniel E. O'Sullivan, 237–46. Boydell and Brewer, 2016.

Robertson, Kellie. "Medieval Things: Materiality, Historicism, and the Premodern Object." *Literature Compass* 5, no. 6 (2008): 1060–80.

Robins, William. "Editing and Evolution." *Literature Compass* 4, no. 1 (2007): 89–120.

Robinson, Michael. "Ornamental Gentlemen: Thomas F. Dibdin, Romantic Bibliomania, and Romantic Sexualities." *European Romantic Review* 22, no. 5 (2011): 685–706.

Robinson, Peter M. W., and Robert J. O'Hara. "Cladistic Analysis of an Old Norse Manuscript Tradition." *Research in Humanities Computing* 4 (1996): 115–37.

Rohy, Valerie. *Lost Causes: Narrative, Etiology, and Queer Theory*. Oxford University Press, 2014.

Rubin, Miri. *Corpus Christi: The Eucharist in Late Medieval Culture*. Cambridge University Press, 1991.

Rudy, Kathryn M. *Piety in Pieces: How Medieval Readers Customized their Manuscripts*. Open Book, 2016.

——. *Postcards on Parchment: The Social Lives of Medieval Books*. Yale University Press, 2015.

——. *Touching Parchment: How Medieval Users Rubbed, Handled, and Kissed their Manuscripts*. 2 vols. Open Book, 2023–2024; volume 3 forthcoming.

——. "Touching the Book Again: The Passional of Abbess Kunigunde of Bohemia." In *Codex und Material*. Edited by Patrizia Carmassi and Gia Toussaint, 247–57. Harrassowitz, 2018.

Rummler, Orion and Kate Sosin. "All the Ways Trump Wants to Exclude Trans People from Public Life." *The 19th**, March 5, 2025. https://19thnews.org/2025/03/trump-anti-trans-executive-orders/, accessed July 15, 2025.

Russell, G. H., and Venetia Nathan. "A *Piers Plowman* Manuscript at the Huntington Library." *Huntington Library Quarterly* 26 (1963): 119–30.

Saenger, Paul. *Space Between Words: The Origins of Silent Reading*. Stanford University Press, 1997.

Salemans, B. J. P. "Building Stemmas with the Computer in a Cladistic, Neo-Lachmannian, Way: The Case of Fourteen Text Versions of *Lanseloet van Denemerken*." PhD diss., Catholic University of Nijmegen, 2000.

Sargan, J. D. "What Could a Trans Book History Look Like? Toward Trans Codicology." *Criticism* 64, no. 3 (2023): 571–86.

Sargent, Michael. "Hidden in Plain Sight: The Obfuscation of Manuscript Evidence in the Modern Critical Edition." In *Dark Archives: Voyages into the Medieval Unread and Unreadable*. Edited by Stephen Pink and Anthony John Lappin, 315–35. Vol. 1. Society for the Study of Medieval Languages and Literature, 2022.

——. "Organic and Cybernetic Metaphors for Manuscript Relations: Stemma – Cladogram – Rhizome – Cloud." In *The Pseudo-Bonaventuran Lives of Christ: Exploring the Middle English Tradition*. Edited by Ian Johnson and Allen E. Westphall, 197–263. Brepols, 2013.

Scase, Wendy. "Two *Piers Plowman* C-Text Interpolations: Evidence for a Second Textual Tradition." *Notes and Queries* n.s. 34, no. 4 (1987): 456–63.

Schlyter, Carl Johan, and Hans Samuel Collin. *Corpus iuris Sueo-Gotorum antiqui*. Vol. 1. Haeggström, 1827.

Schuller, Kyla. *The Biopolitics of Feeling: Race, Sex, and Science in the Nineteenth Century*. Duke University Press, 2018.

Scott, James. *Domination and the Arts of Resistance: Hidden Transcripts*. Yale University Press, 1990.

Sedgwick, Eve Kosofsky. "Paranoid Reading and Reparative Reading; or, You're So Paranoid, You Probably Think This Introduction Is about You." In *Novel Gazing: Queer Readings in Fiction*. Edited by Eve Kosofsky Sedgwick, 1–37. Duke University Press, 1997.

Senchyne, Jonathan. *The Intimacy of Paper in Early and Nineteenth-Century American Literature*. University of Massachusetts Press, 2020.

Sexton, Sophie. "Gender-Queerying Christ's Wounds: A Non-Binary Interpretation of Christ's Body in Late Medieval Imagery." In *Trans and Genderqueer Subjects in Medieval Hagiography*. Edited by Blake Gutt and Alicia Spencer-Hall, 133–53. Amsterdam University Press, 2021.

Simpson, Audra. *Mohawk Interruptus: Political Life Across the Borders of Settler States*. Duke University Press, 2014.

Simpson, Leanne Betasamosake. *As We Have Always Done: Indigenous Freedom Through Radical Resistance*. University of Minnesota Press, 2017.

——. *A Short History of the Blockade: Giant Beavers, Diplomacy, and Regeneration in Nishnaabewin*. University of Alberta Press, 2021.

Smith, Barbara. "Toward a Black Feminist Criticism." *The Radical Teacher*, 7 (1978): 20–27. Reprinted from *Conditions* 1, no. 2 (1977): 25–44.

Somerville, Siobhan. "Scientific Racism, and the Invention of the Homosexual Body." *Journal of the History of Sexuality* 5, no. 2 (1994): 243–66.

Sontag, Susan. "Notes on 'Camp.'" *Partisan Review* 31, no. 4 (1964): 515–30.

Spencer-Hall, Alicia, and Blake Gutt, eds. *Trans and Genderqueer Subjects in Medieval Hagiography*. Amsterdam University Press, 2021.

Spires, Derrick R. "On Liberation Bibliography: The 2021 BSA Annual Meeting Keynote." *PBSA* 116, no. 1 (2022): 1–20.

Spurgeon, Caroline F. E. *Five Hundred Years of Chaucer Criticism and Allusion 1375–1900*. 3 vols. Cambridge University Press, 1925.

——. *Keats's Shakespeare: A Descriptive Study Based on New Material*. Oxford University Press, 1928.

——. *Shakespeare's Imagery, and What it Tells Us*. Cambridge University Press, 1935.

Stahn, Casten. *Confronting Colonial Objects: Histories, Legalities, and Access to Culture*. Oxford University Press, 2023.

Stewart, Columba. "Codicology." HMML School. Hill Museum and Manuscript Library. https://hmmlschool.org/lexicon/14484/, accessed May 26, 2025.

Stoltz, Michael. "Linking the Variance: Unrooted Trees and Networks." In *The Evolution of Texts: Confronting Stemmatological and Genetical Methods*. Edited by Caroline Macé, Philippe Baret, Andrea Bozzi, and Laura Cignoni, 193–213. Instituti Editoriali e Poligrafici Internazionali, 2006.

Strakhov, Elizaveta. "Opening Pandora's Box: Charles d'Orléans's Reception and the Work of Critical Bibliography." *PBSA* 116, no. 4 (2022): 499–535.

Stryker, Susan. "(De)Subjugated Knowledges: An Introduction to Transgender Studies." In *The Transgender Studies Reader*. Edited by Susan Stryker and Stephen Whittle, 1–17. Routledge, 2006.

——. "My Words to Victor Frankenstein above the Village of Chamounix: Performing Transgender Rage." *GLQ: A Journal of Lesbian and Gay Studies* 1, no. 3 (1994): 237–54.

——. *Transgender History*. Seal, 2008.

——. "Transgender History, Homonormativity, and Disciplinarity." *Radical History Review* 100 (2008): 145–57.

——. "Transgender Studies: Queer Theory's Evil Twin." *GLQ: A Journal of Lesbian and Gay Studies* 10, no. 2 (2004): 212–15.

Suarez, Michael F. "Hard Cases: Confronting Bibliographical Difficulty in Eighteenth-Century Texts." *PBSA* 111, no. 1 (2017): 1–30.

Sutherland, Kathryn. "Editing for a New Century: Elizabeth Elstob's Anglo-Saxon Manifesto and Ælfric's St. Gregory Homily." In *The Editing of Old English: Papers from the 1990 Manchester Conference*. Edited by D. G. Scragg and Paul E. Szarmach, 213–37. Boydell, 1994.

——. "Elizabeth Elstob (1683–1756)." In *Medieval Scholarship: Biographical Studies on the Formation of a Discipline: Literature and Philology*. Edited by Helen Damico, 59–73. Routledge, 1998.

Thomas, A. H., ed. *Calendar of Early Mayor's Court Rolls Preserved Among the Archives of the Corporation of London at the Guildhall, A.D. 1298–1307*. Cambridge University Press, 1924.

Toussaint, Gia. *Das Passional der Kunigunde von Böhmen: Bildrhetorik und Spiritualität*. Schöningh, 2003.

Treharne, Elaine. "The Good, the Bad, and the Ugly: Old English Manuscripts and their Physical Description." In *The Genesis of Books: Studies in the Scribal Culture of Medieval England in Honour of A. N. Doane*. Edited by Matthew T. Hussey and John D. Niles, 261–83. Brepols, 2012.

——. *Perceptions of Medieval Manuscripts: The Phenomenal Book*. Oxford University Press, 2021.

Trexler, Richard C. "Gendering Jesus Crucified." In *Iconography at the Crossroads: Papers from the Colloquium Sponsored by the Index of Christian Art, Princeton University, 23–24 March 1990*. Edited by Brendan Cassidy, 107–20. Princeton University, 1993.

Trigg, Stephanie. *Congenial Souls: Reading Chaucer from Medieval to Postmodern*. University of Minnesota Press, 2002.

Truth, Sojourner. "Ain't I A Woman?" *Internet Modern History Sourcebook*. Edited by Paul Halsall. Fordham University, 1997. https://sourcebooks.fordham.edu/mod/sojtruth-woman.asp, accessed July 14, 2025.

Turner, Nancy K. "The Materiality of Medieval Parchment: A Response to the 'Animal Turn.'" *Revista Hispánica moderna* 71, no. 1 (2018): 39–67.

Vaccaro, Jeanne. "Felt Matters." *Women and Performance* 20, no. 3 (2010): 253–66.

Wade, Erik. "Skeletons in the Closet: Scholarly Erasure of Queer and Trans Themes in Early Medieval English Texts." *English Literary History* 89, no. 2 (2022): 281–316.

Wakelin, Daniel. *Designing English: Early Literature on the Page*. Bodleian Library, 2017.

——. *Immaterial Texts in Late Medieval England: Making English Literary Manuscripts, 1400–1500*. Cambridge University Press, 2022.

——. "Paleography." In *The Encyclopedia of Medieval Literature in Britain*. Edited by Siân Echard et al. Wiley, 2017. https://doi.org/10.1002/9781118396957.wbemlb578.

——. *Scribal Correction and Literary Craft: English Manuscripts, 1375–1510*. Cambridge University Press, 2014.

Ward, Jane. "Gender Labor: Transmen, Femmes, and Collective Work of Transgression." *Sexualities* 13, no. 2 (2010): 236–54.

West, Isaac. "Debbie Mayne's Trans/scripts: Performative Repertoires in Law and Everyday Life." *Communication and Critical/Cultural Studies* 5, no. 3 (2008): 245–63.

White, Tom. "National Philology, Imperial Hierarchies, and the 'Defective' Book of Sir John Mandeville." *Review of English Studies* 71, no. 302 (2019): 828–49

Wilson, Georgina. "Surface Reading Paper as Feminist Bibliography." *Criticism* 64, no. 3 (2023): 369–83.

Wingard, Tess. "The Trans Middle Ages: Incorporating Transgender and Intersex Studies into the History of Medieval Sexuality." *English Historical Review* 138, no. 593 (2024): 933–51.

Woloch, Nancy. *The Insider: A Life of Virginia C. Gildersleeve*. Columbia University Press, 2022.

Wood, Sarah. "Nonauthorial *Piers*: C-text Interpolations in the Second Vision of *Piers Plowman* in Huntington Library, MS 114." *Journal of English and Germanic Philology* 114 (2015): 482–503.

Wrathall, John D. "Provenance as Text: Reading the Silences around Sexuality in Manuscript Collections." *The Journal of American History* 79, no. 1 (1992): 165–78.

Wyndham, Diana. *Norman Haire and the Study of Sex*. Sydney University Press, 2012.

Yingst, Carlisle. "Transition by the Book: Editing, Pseudonymity, and the Possibilities of Trans Bibliography." *Papers of the Bibliographical Society of America* 118, no. 2 (2024): 197–222.

Yurcaba, Jo. "Government Agencies Scrub LGBTQ Web Pages and Remove Info about Trans and Intersex People." *NBC News*, February 3, 2025. https://www.nbcnews.com/nbc-out/out-politics-and-policy/government-agencies-scrub-lgbtq-web-pages-remove-info-trans-intersex-p-rcna190519, accessed May 22, 2025.

INDEX

NOTE: Institutions, such as universities and libraries, are listed under their name, not their location.